# *Testimony to the Invisible*

## ESSAYS ON SWEDENBORG

EMANUEL·SWEDENBORG

# *Testimony to the Invisible*

## ESSAYS ON SWEDENBORG

by Jorge Luis Borges

Czeslaw Milosz

Kathleen Raine

D. T. Suzuki

Eugene Taylor

Wilson Van Dusen

Colin Wilson

EDITED BY JAMES F. LAWRENCE

CHRYSALIS BOOKS

IMPRINT OF THE SWEDENBORG FOUNDATION

WEST CHESTER, PENNSYLVANIA

Chrysalis Books is an imprint of the Swedenborg Foundation, Inc. For more in-formation, contact:  Chrysalis Books
Swedenborg Foundation
320 N. Church Street
West Chester, PA 19380

*Library of Congress Cataloging-in-Publication Data*

Testimony to the invisible : essays on Swedenborg / by Jorge Luis Borges . . . [et al.] : edited by James F. Lawrence
    p.        cm.
    ISBN 0-87785-149-2
    1. Swedenborg, Emanuel, 1688–1772.    I. Borges, Jorge Luis, 1899–1986.
II. Lawrence, James F., 1955–.
BX8711.T47      1995                                            95–20167
289.4'092—dc20                        .                              CIP

Illustrations from The Bettman Archive, New York, NY: Jorge Luis Borges, p. 2; Czeslaw Milosz, p. 18; Fyodor Dostoevsky, p. 27; William Blake, p. 50; Ralph Waldo Emerson, p. 156.
Picture of D.T. Suzuki, p. 172, by Francis Haar, Courtesy of Tom Haar Photogra-phy, Honolulu, HI.

Edited by Mary Lou Bertucci
Designed by Joanna V. Hill
Typeset in Cochin and Baskerville by Ruttle, Shaw & Wetherill, Inc.

# *Contents*

# Introduction

BY JAMES F. LAWRENCE

Serious students of Emanuel Swedenborg frequently marvel at the sweeping impact the Swedish visionary's provocative ideas have had on creative and significant contributors to modern cultural thought across numerous artistic and philosophic disciplines throughout most of modern civilization. Beyond such standard references as William Blake and Ralph Waldo Emerson, a vast international coterie of characters continues popping up, once Swedenborg has been lodged in one's conscious awareness: D. T. Suzuki; Sadhu Sundar Singh; Johann Wolfgang von Goethe; Honoré de Balzac; Fyodor Dostoevsky; W. B. Yeats; Edgar Allen Poe; August Strindberg; Johann Friedrich Oberlin; Immanuel Kant; Charles Bauderlaire; George Washington; Abraham Lincoln; Robert and Elizabeth Barrett Browning; Samuel Taylor Coleridge; Czeslaw Milosz; Helen Keller; Carl Jung; Ping Chong; and, of course, the lead essayist for the present volume, Jorge Luis Borges. The creative cross-pollinating perspectives on Swedenborg's presence within the very fabric of modern thought is circuit-blowing.

How is it that the writings of a celebrated scientist-cum-Christian prophet can engage the imagination and creatively commingle within the work of such grandly diverse personalities as the leading exponent of Zen in America, the philosophic titan of Transcendentalism, the trailblazing lion of modern Latin and South American literature, and the brooding Nobel Prize-winning poet from Eastern Europe? This collection of essays plumbs some of the depths and shoots some of the necessary heights needed to gain the proper perspective upon the system of spiritual philosophy within Swedenborg's life work that enables him to appeal to physicists and poets, statesmen and artists.

The lead essay is by a literary figure many believe to be the foremost spiritual voice emanating this century from South America—short-story master, poet, essayist, and metaphysician Jorge Luis Borges. Though he shared the International Editor's Prize with Samuel Beckett in 1961 and was awarded the Annual Literary Award by the Ingram Merrill Foundation in 1966, many critics feel his failure to receive the Nobel Prize for literature to be an outrageous oversight.

Nevertheless, for the past thirty years, Borges's fiction has established him as the modern master short-story writer in the Spanish language. So striking is his imagery and stylistic devices, he is generally credited with creating a new genre of fiction. As a literary icon to millions, his final place in world literature is yet to be reckoned.

Born in 1899 in Buenos Aires of Spanish, English, Portuguese, and Jewish blood, Borges's eventual cosmopolitanism perhaps could have been predicted. His first language was English; but, for the last several decades of his life, he wrote only in Spanish. Borges was raised in a sheltered environment and was encouraged to pursue his intellectual interests, which largely veered into philosophy and literature. After World War I, Borges and his family spent two years in Spain, where he launched his literary career. There he found a new philosophical movement among a young rebellious group of intellectuals. Called the Ultraist Movement, they rebelled against classicism in both form and content and drew upon radically free verse, heavy use of metaphor, and injection of much absurd humor to make their points.

Borges returned to Buenos Aires in 1921 and quickly became the leading exponent in South America of Ultraist literature. But it wasn't until the 1940s and 1950s that he stumbled onto the genre that would establish his fame. On Christmas Eve, 1938, Borges struck his head against a recently painted open window. Lead poisoning developed from the wound, and Borges suddenly hovered near death for several weeks. Upon recovering, he found himself obsessed by a fear of lost creative powers. He decided to write a short story, reasoning that failure in a genre for which he was less known would be less humiliating. The result was *Pierre Menard, Author of Don Quijote*, one of his most praised works. His "tragedy" had led him to the medium in which he would make his farthest-reaching contributions.

For the next twenty years, Borges forged an art form for fiction in Latin and South America that set a new standard and a new landscape. Displaying provocative stylistic innovations and drawing extensively upon metaphysical imagery, his stories are more in the vein of Franz Kafka, Poe, and I.B. Singer—yet with a distinctively explicit use of spiritually esoteric ideas and images. Borges, who became fully blind in 1955, often invokes Chinese mysticism, the cabala, and other standard mystical references into his stories, as well as building entire story structures within surreal planes.

Borges's interest in Swedenborg deepened as part of his growing fascination with mystical states of knowing. In a lecture delivered at the University of Belgrano (Buenos Aires), he stated, "Voltaire said that Charles XII was the most extraordinary man recorded by history. I would say—if we admit such superlatives—the most extraordinary man was the most mysterious of the subjects of Charles XII, Emanuel Swedenborg." The title essay for this volume was originally written as the introduction to a Spanish edition of *The Essential Swedenborg* by Sig Synnestedt. Borges attempts to trace the outlines of Swedenborg's intellectual and spiritual development and displays his specialized interest in Swedenborg's ability to experience lucid inner states and worlds of heaven and hell.

Borges professes his profound admiration of Swedenborg's mode of knowing in this essay, and one quickly discerns that he also feels a kindred spirit to the Swedish mystic. Borges declares that he himself is not a mystic, but that mysticism is an important and fascinating subject for him. When the epistemology of the knower is of solid pedigree, he believed, then the ensuing perceptions are the most sublime humanity has known. Borges felt that he shared with Swedenborg the same fundamental objectives; they simply traversed the same terrain in somewhat different ways.

Borges believed in Swedenborg's spiritual journeys more profoundly than many artists and poets who have expressed perhaps some admiration or inspiration but who have not been so deeply inclined to explore the same realities with as much conviction and daring as Borges. It is in this sense that Borges was most deeply Swedenborgian.

A figure looming both directly and indirectly throughout these essays is William Blake. Borges himself confessed to a deep and abiding interest in Blake's mysticism; three other contributors to this volume—Czeslaw Milosz, Kathleen Raine, and Colin Wilson—also cite Blake as a seminal force in their work. When, as a young man, he came upon Blake's searing imaginative works, Wilson immersed himself into everything Blake wrote; and Raine, whose essay centers on Blake's debt to Swedenborg, says flatly in an interview with *Gnosis* magazine in 1992: "Blake is my master." Milosz counts Blake as one of just five foundational influences on his work. Two others, Swedenborg and Dostoevsky, are the subjects of his essay in this collection.

Czeslaw Milosz, accorded the highest honor in literature in 1980, the Nobel Prize, has lived in Berkeley, California, since 1961, when he joined the faculty of the University of California, where today he is professor emeritus of Slavic languages and literature. Lithuanian by birth and Polish by upbringing, Milosz, like Borges, is a man of many languages, who, nonetheless, does not write in English. He speaks and/or reads Russian, French, Lithuanian, Greek, Hebrew, and Polish, the language of his art.

As a young man, Milosz was a staunch Communist who became virulently anti-Nazi, having watched at the age of 28 his beloved Warsaw devastated by the German blitzkrieg. After the war ended, he worked for a time with the Soviet-backed puppet government in Poland but soon came to realize "all the horrible lies of communism." In fact, until he won the Nobel Prize, Milosz was probably best known in this country for a seminal work of political philosophy, *The Captive Mind*, a brilliant treatise on the insidiousness of totalitarianism.

While Milosz has never worn comfortably the mantle of political expositor, his poetry cannot be understood outside the context of war, oppression, and of the brutalities, both physical and psychological, he has personally observed in his lifetime. In many poems, he betrays the anxiety and uncertainty of an existentialist, but then he turns around and writes with the fire of a prophet. Significantly, Milosz ultimately chooses the perspective of meaning and purpose when surveying the human condition. His final message is one of salvation—perhaps an elusive but a substantially real possibility of spiritual redemption.

Milosz's confessed list of five mentors reveals the creative tension between existentialist concerns and mystical solutions: Dostoevsky and Simone Weil, on the one hand; Blake, Swedenborg, and Oscar de la Milosz, on the other. In his newly released diary chronicling the 77th year of his life, *A Year of the Hunter*, Milosz invokes one of his favorite quotes by the poet Maurice Maeterlinck: "Lord, I did what I could. Is it my fault thou didst not speak more clearly? I tried my best to understand." His essay in this collection, "Dostoevsky and Swedenborg," is an excellent example of Milosz's attempt to resolve the philosophic tension inherent in Milosz's worldview by harmonizing the insights not only of Swedenborg and Dostoevsky but also of Blake, whom he cites as the one who really understood Swedenborg.

Kathleen Raine, considered by many to be the foremost

living female poet in Great Britain, is also recognized as a leading Blakean scholar, her two-volume *William Blake* (1970) being a standard reference in the field. In her essay in this volume, "The Human Face of God," she highlights prominent theological propositions driving much of Blake's most celebrated works and shows Blake, for all his originality and imagination, to be peculiarly Swedenborgian in the most fundamental aspects of his worldview.

Raine also helps to put Blake's famed rebelliousness against Swedenborg into perspective, demonstrating that his deepest Swedenborgian sympathies can be found in his later works; that, after his early enthusiasm had given way to mid-life reconsideration, Blake climbed onto a final plane of new vision for Swedenborg's cosmologies and understood Swedenborg's vision all anew. This is fortunate for contemporary Swedenborg students, she avers, pointing out that ". . . unawares, the teachings of Swedenborg's Church of the New Jerusalem have permeated the spiritual sensibility of the English nation, through Blake."

Colin Wilson is the other British writer featured in this collection. He holds a unique position among serious authors of spirituality in the United Kingdom: never an academic, he yet is appealed to as an expert by the general public. As a best-selling author for twenty-five years, he has done more than any other to make esotericism in thought and practice not only respectable but popular in that nation.

Leaping upon the scene in 1956 as a precocious 24-year-old sage with a smash first book, *The Outsider,* which stayed on the bestseller lists on both sides of the Atlantic for many months and is still regarded not only as a classic but as a kind of underground manifesto, Wilson seems to have inherited the mantle as the chief spokesperson on themes related to contemporary spirituality. He appears frequently on television and radio interviews.

From the beginning, Swedenborg has been a figure of significant interest for Wilson. He discussed the clairvoyant Swedish scientist-theologian in *The Outsider*; but, in his next book, *Religion and the Rebel* (1957), Wilson gave Swedenborg an entire chapter. In 1978, he wrote an extensive piece on Swedenborg as an introduction to a new translation of Swedenborg's own "bestseller" *Heaven and Hell*; it is this essay that appears in the present volume. Wilson demonstrates an especial interest in Swedenborg's unique mode of visionary consciousness. A lifelong student of the paranormal, Wilson attempts to plumb the nature of Swedenborg's inner states and provides possible perspectives for gaining a partial understanding of Swedenborg's personal psychological dimensions.

Significantly, Wilson draws upon the work of another contributor to this collection, the psychologist and interpreter of Swedenborg Wilson Van Dusen, author of the most widely read book on Swedenborg written in the twentieth century, *The Presence of Other Worlds*.

Van Dusen displays an unusual facility with and respect for Swedenborg's various modes of mystical consciousness. As the title to his essay "A Mystic Looks at a Mystic" indicates, Van Dusen's uncanny sensitivity comes from a sense of traveling sympathetically similar realms, but also from a conviction gained from insights gleaned from his own professional career. As the chief psychologist at Mendocino State Mental Hospital for twenty years, Van Dusen developed a reputation for highly original and successful work with schizophrenic patients, not unlike that of R. D. Laing. Van Dusen's discussion of the psychological aspects of Swedenborg's consciousness is approached not only with empathy but with considerable sophistication.

Other than William Blake, no other great figure in the cultural heritage of the English-speaking world is more colored with a Swedenborgian tinge than is Ralph Waldo Emerson. Our contributor, Eugene Taylor, is distinguished as a leading scholar on William James and as a searching writer on ideas intrinsic to the far-reaching spiritual movement known as Transcendentalism, both of which owe a profound debt to Swedenborg. In a lively essay chock-full of connecting references, Taylor convincingly provides the underpinnings of both Emerson's and the Transcendentalist movement's development in the light of Swedenborg's direct and indirect influence.

Finally, a poetic voice of another style is brought to this collection by D. T. Suzuki. A master scholar of Zen, Suzuki's interest in Swedenborg is particularly welcome, not only because it brings an important Eastern voice into the cross-cultural forum but also because readers of Swedenborg recently have awakened to a Zen-like wisdom at the base of his involved metaphysical theology. Although it was William Blake who once declared that Swedenborg believed in "salvation by understanding," there is much in Swedenborg that is about *being*. Indeed, another author in our collection, Wilson Van Dusen, has explored a Zen-like state of enlightenment that occurs when one attains the Swedenborgian goal of feeling the divine goodness in the act of aware usefulness—a co-creative experience of God in "the now."*

---

*Wilson Van Dusen, *Uses: A Way of Personal and Spiritual Growth* (West Chester, PA: The Swedenborg Foundation, 1978; rpt. 1987).

Suzuki became fascinated with Swedenborg as an example of a Western mystic whose mind was both productive and enlightened, but he was equally interested in the contributions Swedenborg could make to the East in understanding spiritual principles. Indeed, as is mentioned elsewhere in this book, it is instructive to note that, just as Suzuki is regarded as the one who introduced Westerners to Zen, he is also known as the one who introduced the Japanese to Swedenborg. Suzuki's enduring legacy is both as a brilliant scholar of Zen, specializing in a dialogue with the West, and as a Zen practitioner with a unique gift for articulating pithy insights—not unlike Emerson's position among the historical legends of philosophy. His place in Buddhist scholarship is generally held to be as the most effective Zen Buddhist writer influencing Western patterns of thinking, actually sparking deep interest in Zen concepts.

Suzuki's strongest criticism of the Western mind was the unmooring from an integrated beingness in the "now" caused by the supremacy of analytical thinking over a basic experience of the totality, the oneness possible prior to the split caused by the experience of analysis—especially that between subject and object. Suzuki said that "Zen teaches us to go beyond logic and not to tarry even when we come up against 'the things which are not seen.'" He repeatedly emphasized the necessity of awakening to a high, intuitive knowing before the separation between self and other, which conveys a connection to deep reality and, with that, peace and healing.

In Swedenborg, Suzuki found a Christian mystic who, though analytical in the best of the Western tradition, worked from an inner spiritual center that was *a priori* to his deep mental work—and that was the reason he was able to traverse the divide between the spiritual and the natural so matter-of-factly. Suzuki believed that Swedenborg accomplished the unity of mind/spirit that the analytical West so desperately needed—and this by one of the West's greatest analytical scientists! In his famed lunch in 1954 with Mircea Eliade and Suzuki, Islamic scholar Henry Corbin relates that, when asked to compare Swedenborgian and Buddhist insights, "Suzuki suddenly brandished a spoon and [said] with a smile: 'This spoon *now* exists in Paradise!'"

From 1909–1915, Suzuki involved himself in a rigorous study of Swedenborg, whom he referred to as "the Buddha of the North," translating four volumes of Swedenborg's writings into Japanese and also writing his own concise book, *Suedenborugu* (1913). Kei Torita, an ordained Swedenborgian minister living in Tokyo, has translated and reconstructed, with the editorial help of Mary Lou Bertucci, the gist from Suzuki's commentary on Swedenborg into a seamless essay.

This collection of writings on Swedenborg from some of the most celebrated writers of the twentieth century comes to us from East and West, North and South, from poets and psychologists, historians and philosophers. Together, they provide one illuminating perspective after another onto the massive prism that is Emanuel Swedenborg. They see brilliant colors and forms from such different angles—yet all appear to see aspects of the same light.

# *Testimony to the Invisible*

## ESSAYS ON SWEDENBORG

JORGE LUIS BORGES

# Testimony
# to the Invisible

## BY JORGE LUIS BORGES

Translated by Catherine Rodriguez-Nieto

In his famous lecture of 1845, Ralph Waldo Emerson cited Emanuel Swedenborg as a classic example of the mystic. This word, while it is extremely accurate, runs the risk of suggesting a man apart, a man who instinctively removes himself from the circumstances and urgencies we call, though I will never know why, reality. No one is further from that image than Emanuel Swedenborg, who journeyed, lucid and laborious, through this and all other worlds. No one accepted life more fully, no one investigated it with a passion so great, with the same intellectual love, or with such impatience to learn about it. No one was less like a monk than that sanguine Scandinavian who went much farther than Eric the Red.

Like the Buddha, Swedenborg rejected asceticism, which impoverishes men and can diminish them. Within the boundaries of heaven, he saw a hermit who had set out to gain admittance there and had voluntarily spent his mortal life in the solitude of the desert. Having reached his goal, the blessed one discovers that he is unable to follow the conversation of the angels or fathom the complexities of paradise. He is finally permitted to project around himself a hallucinatory image of the wilderness. There he remains, as he did on earth, engaged in self-denial and prayer but without the hope of reaching heaven.

Jesper Swedberg, Emanuel's father, was an eminent Lutheran bishop, in whom fervor and tolerance existed in rare conjunction. Emanuel was born in Stockholm near the beginning of 1688. From early childhood, he thought about God and actively sought conversation with the clerics who frequented his father's house. It is not insignificant that he placed above salvation through faith—the cornerstone of the reform preached by Luther—salvation through good works, which is irrefutable evidence of the former. This peerless, solitary man was many men. He did not scorn craftsmanship; as a youth in London, he practiced the manual arts as bookbinder, cabinetmaker, optician, watchmaker, manufacturer of scientific instruments, and engraver of maps for globes. All of this he accomplished without neglecting the discipline of the various natural sciences, algebra, and the new astronomy of Sir Isaac Newton, with whom he would have liked to converse but whom he never met. His application was always inventive; he anticipated the nebular theory of [Pierre Simon de] Laplace and [Immanuel] Kant and designed a craft capable of flight and another, for military purposes, that could navigate below the surface of the ocean. We are indebted to him for a personal method of fixing longitudes and a treatise on the diameter of the moon. Toward 1716 he began publication in Uppsala of a scientific journal beautifully titled *Daedalus Hyperboreus*, which would continue to appear for two years. His aversion to purely speculative endeavor caused him, in 1717, to refuse the chair in astronomy offered him by the Swedish king. During the reckless and quasi-mythical wars waged by Karl XII, he served as a military engineer. He conceived and constructed a device to move boats over a stretch of land more than fourteen miles long. In 1734 his three-volume *Opera Philosophica et Mineralia* appeared in Saxony. He wrote good Latin hexameters and was interested in English literature—Spenser, Shakespeare, Cowley, Milton, and Dryden—because of its imaginative power. Even had he not consecrated himself to mysticism, his name would be illustrious in the annals of science. Like René Descartes, he was interested in the problem of the precise point at which the soul is connected to the body. Anatomy, physics, algebra, and chemistry inspired the many works he wrote, following the custom of his time, in Latin. In Holland he was struck by the faith and well-being of the inhabitants; he attributed them to the country's being a republic because, in kingdoms, the people, accustomed to adulating the king, also adulate God, a servile characteristic that cannot please him. We should note in passing that, during his journeys, Swedenborg visited schools, universities, poor neighborhoods, and factories; and was fond of music, particularly opera. He served as assessor to the Royal Board of Mines and sat in the House of Nobles [of the Riksdag]. He always preferred the study of sacred scripture to that of dogmatic theology. Latin translations were not good enough for him; he studied the original texts in Hebrew and Greek. In a private diary, he accuses himself of monstrous pride; while leafing through the volumes that lined the shelves of a bookstore, it occurred to him that he could, without much

effort, improve on them, and then understood that the
Lord has a thousand ways of touching the human heart
and that there is no such thing as a useless book. Pliny the
Younger had written that no book is so bad there is nothing good in it, an opinion Miguel Cervantes would recall.

The most important event of Swedenborg's human life
took place in London, one night in April 1745. He himself called it the "discrete degree" or the "degree of separation." It was preceded by dreams, prayer, periods of
doubt, fasting, and—much more surprisingly—by diligent
scientific and philosophical work. A stranger who had
silently followed him through the streets of London, and
about whose looks nothing is known, suddenly appeared
in his room and told him that he was the Lord.[1] He immediately entrusted to Swedenborg the mission of revealing to men, by then sunk in atheism, error, and sin, the
true, lost faith of Jesus. He announced to him that his
spirit would travel through heavens and hells and that he
would be able to converse with the dead, with demons,
and with angels.

The chosen one was then fifty-seven years old; during
nearly thirty years more, he led the life of a visionary,
which he recorded in closely reasoned treatises written in
clear, unequivocal prose. Unlike other mystics, he es-
chewed metaphor, exaltation, and vague, fiery hyperbole.

The explanation is obvious. The use of any word what-
soever presupposes a shared experience, for which the
word is the symbol. If someone speaks to us about the fla-

---

1. So far as can be ascertained, Borges's account of a man following Swedenborg around the streets of London and then appearing to him as the Lord is a
totally original one.—*Editor*

vor of coffee, it is because we have already tasted it; if about the color yellow, because we have already seen lemons, gold, wheat, and sunsets. To suggest the ineffable union of man's soul with the divine being, the Sufis of Islam found themselves obliged to resort to prodigious analogies, to images of roses, intoxication, or carnal love. Swedenborg was able to abstain from this kind of rhetorical artifice because his subject matter was not the ecstasy of a rapt and fainting soul but, rather, the accurate description of regions that, though ultraterrestrial, were clearly defined. In order for us to imagine, or to begin to imagine, the lowest depth of hell, John Milton speaks to us of "No light, but rather darkness visible." Swedenborg prefers the rigor and—why not say it?—possible wordiness of the explorer or geographer who is recording unknown kingdoms.

As I dictate these lines,[2] I feel the reader's incredulity holding me back like a high, bronze wall, buttressed by two assumptions: deliberate imposture on the part of the man who wrote such strange things or the influence of sudden or progressive madness. The first is inadmissible. Had Emanuel Swedenborg intended to deceive, he would not have resorted to anonymous publication of a good part of his work, as he did for the nine volumes of his *Arcana Coelestia,* which do not avail themselves of the authority conferred by his already illustrious name. We know that he was not proselytizing in the dialogue. Like Emerson and Walt Whitman, he believed that arguments

2. This essay was dictated by Borges, who was blind, to his secretary to be used as a prologue to the Spanish edition of Sig Synnestvedt's *The Essential Swedenborg* (Swedenborg Foundation, 1977).—*Editor*

persuade no one and that stating a truth is sufficient for its acceptance by those who hear it. He always shunned polemic. There is not one syllogism in his entire work, only terse, tranquil affirmations. I am referring, of course, to his mystical treatises.

The hypothesis of madness is equally unfounded. If the writer of *Daedalus Hyperboreus* and *Prodromus Principiorum Rerum Naturalium* had gone mad, we would not owe to his tenacious pen the thousands of methodical pages he wrote during the following thirty years or so, pages that have nothing at all to do with frenzy.

Let us consider now his coherent multiple visions, which certainly contain much that is miraculous. William White[3] has observed with acuity that we docilely surrender our faith to the visions of the ancients, while tending to reject or ridicule those of the moderns. We believe in Ezekiel because he is exalted by remoteness in time and space: we believe in Saint John of the Cross because he is an integral part of Spanish literature; but we do not believe in William Blake, Swedenborg's rebellious disciple, or in his master, still near to us in time. Edward Gibbon said the same of miracles. Exactly when did true visions cease and apocryphal ones begin?

Swedenborg devoted two years to the study of Hebrew in order to examine scripture directly. I personally believe—and it must be understood that this is the opinion, doubtless heterodox, of a mere man of letters and not a researcher or theologian—that Swedenborg, like [Benedictus de] Spinoza or Francis Bacon, was a thinker in his

---

3. William White was a nineteenth-century biographer of Swedenborg.— *Editor*

own right who made an awkward mistake when he decided to adapt his ideas to the framework of the two Testaments. This had happened to the Hebrew Cabalists, who were essentially neoplatonists when they invoked the authority of the verses, words, and even letters and transpositions of letters in Genesis to justify their system.

It is not my intent to expound the doctrine of the New Jerusalem revealed by Swedenborg, but I do want to dwell on two points. The first is his extremely original concept of heaven and hell, which he explains at length in the best known and most beautiful of his treatises, *De Coelo et Inferno*, published in Amsterdam in 1758. Blake repeats it and Bernard Shaw vividly summarized it in the third act of *Man and Superman* (1903), in the narration of John Tanner's dream. Shaw never, so far as I know, spoke of Swedenborg; it might be supposed that he wrote under the stimulus of Blake, whom he mentions frequently and with respect; nor is it impossible to believe that he arrived at the same ideas independently.

In a famous letter to Cangrande Della Scala, Dante Alighieri points out that his *Commedia*, like Sacred Scripture, can be read four different ways, of which the literal way is only one. But the reader, in the thrall of the splendid poetry, forms an indelible impression that the nine circles of hell, the nine terraces of purgatory, and the nine heavens of paradise correspond to three establishments: one whose nature is penal; one, penitential; and another—if the neologism is allowable—premial. Passages such as *Lasciate ogni speranza, voi ch'entrate* ("All hope abandon, ye who enter here") reinforce the topographical conviction created through art. Nothing is farther from the ultraterrestrial destinations of Swedenborg. The heaven and hell of his doctrine are not places, even though the souls of the dead who inhabit and, in a way, create them perceive them as being situated in space. They are conditions of the soul, determined by its former life. Heaven is forbidden to no one; hell, imposed on no one. The doors, so to speak, are open. People who have died but fail to realize they are dead project, for an indefinite period of time, an illusory image of their customary ambiance and of the people who surrounded them. At the end of that period, strangers approach them. The wicked dead find the looks and manner of demons to be agreeable and quickly join them; the righteous choose angels. For the blessed, the diabolical sphere is a region full of swamps, caves, burning huts, ruins, brothels, and taverns. The damned are faceless or their features are mutilated, atrocious (in the eyes of the righteous); but they believe themselves to be beautiful. For them, happiness lies in the exercise of power and in mutual hatred. They devote their lives to politics, in the most South American sense of the word: that is, they live to scheme, to lie, and to impose their will on others. Swedenborg recounts that a ray of celestial light once fell into the depths of hell; the damned perceived it as stench, as an ulcerated wound, and as darkness.

Hell is the other face of heaven. Its exact opposite is necessary for the balance of creation. The Lord rules over it as he does over heaven. Balance between the two spheres is required for free will, which must unceasingly choose between good, which emanates from heaven, and evil, which emanates from hell. Every day, every instant of every day, man is shaping his eternal damnation or his salvation. We will be what we are. The terrors or anxieties of agony, which usually occur when a dying person is frightened and confused, are of little importance. Whether we believe in the immortality of the soul or not, we must recognize that the doctrine revealed by Swedenborg is more moral and reasonable than one that postulates a mysterious gift gotten, almost by chance, at the eleventh hour. To begin with, it leads us to the practice of virtue in our lives.

Innumerable heavens constitute the heaven Swedenborg saw; innumerable angels constitute each heaven, and each angel is, individually, a heaven. All are ruled by an ardent love of God and neighbor. The overall shape of heaven (and of the heavens) is the shape of a man or, what amounts to the same thing, that of an angel, because angels are not a separate species. Angels, like demons, are the dead who have passed into the angelic or demonic sphere. A curious stroke, suggesting the fourth dimension contemplated by Henry More: angels, wherever they may be, are always directly facing the Lord. In the spiritual sphere, the sun is the visible image of God. Space and time exist only as illusions; if one person thinks of another, the second is immediately at the side of the first. The angels converse like men, through spoken words that are enunciated and heard; but the language they use is natural and need not be learned. It is common to all the angelic spheres. The art of writing is not unknown in heaven; more than once, Swedenborg received divine communications that seemed to be handwritten or printed but that he was unable to decipher completely because the Lord prefers direct, oral instruction. Regardless of baptism, regardless of the religion professed by their parents, all children go to heaven, where they are taught by the angels. Neither riches, nor happiness, nor luxury, nor worldly life is a barrier to entering heaven. To be poor has no merit; it is no virtue, any more than is the suffering of misfortune. Good will and the love of God are essential; external circumstances are not. We have already seen the case of the hermit who, through self-mortification and solitude, made himself unfit for heaven and was obliged to forgo its delights.

In his treatise on conjugial love, which appeared in 1768, Swedenborg says that marriage is never perfect on earth because understanding predominates in men and will predominates in women. In the celestial state, a man and woman who have loved one another will form a single angel.

In the Apocalypse, one of the canonical books of the New Testament, Saint John of Patmos speaks of a heavenly Jerusalem; Swedenborg extends this idea to other great cities. Thus, in *Vera Christiana Religio* (1771), he writes that there are two ultraterrestrial Londons. When men die, they do not lose their character. The English preserve the intimate light of their intellect and their respect for authority; the Dutch continue to engage in commerce; Germans are usually loaded down with books, and, when someone asks them a question, they consult the appropriate volume before answering. Moslems present the most curious case of all. Because the concepts of Mohammed and religion are inextricably intertwined in their souls, God provides them with an angel who pretends to be Mohammed to teach them. This is not always the same angel. The real Mohammed emerged once before the community of the faithful just long enough to say the words, "I am your Mohammed," before turning back and sinking back into hell.

There are no hypocrites in the spiritual sphere; each person is what he is. An evil spirit ordered Swedenborg to write that it is the delight of demons to commit adultery, robbery, and fraud, and to lie; and they also delight in the stench of excrement and dead bodies. I am abridging this episode; the curious may consult the last page of the treatise *Sapientia Angelica de Divina Providentia* ( 1764).

Unlike the heaven referred to by other visionaries, Swedenborg's heaven is more precise than earth. Shapes, objects, structures, and colors are more complex and vivid. In the Gospels, salvation is an ethical process. Righteousness is fundamental; humility, misery, and misfortune are also exalted. To the requirement of righteousness, Swedenborg adds another, never before mentioned by any theologian: intelligence. Let us again remember the ascetic who was forced to recognize that he was unworthy of the theological conversation of the angels. (The incalculable heavens of Swedenborg are full of love and theology.) When Blake writes, "The fool shall not enter into Glory, no matter how holy he may be," [*El tonto no entrará en la Gloria, por santo que sea*] or "Strip yourselves of sanctity and clothe yourselves in intelligence," [*Despojáos de santidad y cubríos de inteligencia*], he is doing nothing more than minting laconic epigrams from the discursive thought of Swedenborg. Blake also affirms that the salvation of man demands a third requirement: that he be an artist. Jesus Christ was an artist because he taught through parables and metaphor rather than abstract reasoning.

It is not without misgiving that I turn now to outline, albeit partially and in a rudimentary fashion, the doctrine

of correspondences, which for many is central to the subject we are studying. In the Middle Ages, it was thought
that the Lord had written two books, one of which we call
the Bible and the other of which we call the universe. It
was our duty to interpret them. I suspect that Swedenborg
began with the exegesis of the first. He conjectured that
each word of Scripture has a spiritual sense and eventually
prepared a vast system of hidden meanings. Stones, for
example, represent natural truths; precious stones, spiritual truths; stars, divine knowledge; the horse, a correct
understanding of Scripture but also its distortion through
sophistry; the abomination of desolation, the Trinity; the
abyss, God or hell; etc.

From a symbolic reading of the Bible, Swedenborg
would have gone on to a symbolic reading of the universe
and of human beings. The sun in the sky is an image of
the spiritual sun, which is, in turn, an image of God.
There is not a single creature on earth that does not owe
its continued existence to the constant influence of the
Divine Being. Thomas De Quincey, who was a reader of
Swedenborg's works, writes that the smallest things are
secret mirrors of the greatest. Thomas Carlyle says that
universal history is a text we must continually read and
write, and in which we are also written. The disturbing
suspicion that we are ciphers and symbols in a divine
cryptography whose true meaning we do not know
abounds in the volumes of Leon Bloy, and the Jewish
Cabalists knew of it.

The doctrine of correspondences has brought me to
mention the Cabala. No one whom I know of or remember has yet investigated its intimate affinity. In the first
chapter of Scripture, we read that God created man ac-

cording to his own image and likeness. This affirmation implies that God has the shape of a man. The Cabalists who compiled the *Book of Creation* declare that the ten emanations, or *sefiroth*, whose source is the ineffable divinity, can be conceived under the species of a tree or of a man, the primordial man, the Adam Kadmon. If all things are in God, all things will be in man, who is his earthly reflection. Thus, Swedenborg and the Cabala both arrive at the concept of the microcosm, that is to say, man as the mirror or compendium of the universe. According to Swedenborg, hell and heaven are in man, as well as plants, mountains, seas, continents, minerals, trees, flowers, thistles, fish, tools, cities, and buildings.

In 1758, Swedenborg announced that the previous year he had witnessed the Last Judgment, which had taken place in the world of the spirits on the exact date when faith was extinguished in all the churches. The decline began when the church of Rome was founded. The reform undertaken by Martin Luther and prefigured by John Wycliffe was imperfect and often heretical. Another Last Judgment takes place at the moment of each man's death; it is the consequence of his entire former life.

On 29 March 1772, Emanuel Swedenborg died in London, the city he so loved, the city in which God had one night entrusted to him the mission that would make him unique among men. Some testimonials remain of his last days, of his ancient black velvet suit, and of a sword with a strangely shaped hilt.

His way of life was austere during his last years; his nourishment consisted of only coffee, milk, and bread. The servants could hear him at any hour of the day or night walking to and fro in his bedroom, conversing with his angels.

Sometime around 1970, I wrote this sonnet:

EMANUEL SWEDENBORG

Taller than the others, this man
Walked among them, at a distance,
Now and then calling the angels
By their secret names. He would see
That which earthly eyes do not see:
The fierce geometry, the crystal
Labyrinth of God and the sordid
Milling of infernal delights.
He knew that Glory and Hell too
Are in your soul, with all their myths;
He knew, like the Greek, that the days
Of time are Eternity's mirrors.
In dry Latin he went on listing
The unconditional Last Things.[4]

4. Translated by Richard Howard and Cesar Rennert.

CZESLAW MILOSZ

# Dostoevsky
# and Swedenborg

## BY CZESLAW MILOSZ.

Translated by Louis Iribarne

Very few books and studies on Dostoevsky appeared in the first two decades after his death. The year 1900 may be chosen as the turning point; after that date, the number of publications, first in Russian and then in other languages, increased steadily. By the middle of our century, the canon of Dostoevsky scholarship was well established, so that hardly any new departures seemed to be possible. Today, whether our attention is focused on Dostoevsky's opinions or upon the stylistic devices and structures of his novels, we note that practically every method of approach has already been tried by at least one of our predecessors. Thus Dostoevsky, not unlike Nietzsche, was discovered and appropriated by the first half of the twentieth century. It was then that he grew to the stature he now possesses, and it was then that he was recognized as a forerunner of new trends in European literature and philosophy.

Seen from the present, as the past recedes in time, it is quite normal for the perspective to change and for some habits of thought once accepted as universal to reveal their conventional character. These habits explain certain blind spots or unintentional omissions, while new questions arise concerning Dostoevsky's significance as a historical phenomenon. This essay toys with some interpretations of Dostoevsky that may be applied in the future, when the present transitional stage is over. It introduces the name of Emanuel Swedenborg as a useful catalyst.

Swedenborg may be linked with Dostoevsky in two ways. First, Russia's cultural lag left the Russian intelligentsia open to a sudden onslaught of Western scientific thinking, with centuries compressed into a few decades. That is why Dostoevsky the religious thinker is similar in many respects to religious thinkers in the West who earlier resisted the corroding impact of scientific innovations. Not infrequently, he resembles and even sounds like Pascal. In the seventeenth century, Pascal was, after all, the most representative of those writers engaged in the defense of the faith against the skeptics. Also, the Age of Reason, as personified by Voltaire, oppressed Dostoevsky, as did nineteenth-century science, personified for him by Claude Bernard ("Bernardy" in *The Brothers Karamazov*). As a theologian confronted with the rationalistic science of the day, Swedenborg had recourse to an aggressive exegesis of Christianity, and an analogous tendency can be distinguished in Dostoevsky.

A second link is provided by Dostoevsky's borrowings from Swedenborg. To affirm that they exist is not far-fetched, for even the books in Dostoevsky's library supply a sort of material proof. The catalog of Dostoevsky's library, published in 1922 by Leonid Grossman,[1] lists three such books. These are, all in Russian, the following: A. N. Aksakov, *The Gospel according to Swedenborg: Five Chapters of the Gospel of John with an Exposition and a Discussion of Their Spiritual Meaning according to the Teaching on Correspondences* (Leipzig, 1864); A. N. Aksakov, *On Heaven, the World of Spirits and on Hell, as They Were Seen and Heard by Swedenborg,* translation from the Latin (Leipzig, 1863); A. N. Aksakov, *The Rationalization of Swedenborg: A Critical Analysis of His Teaching on the Holy Writ* (Leipzig, 1870). A. N. Aksakov was in Russia a chief proponent of spiritism or, as we would say today, parapsychology—an interest that was treated unkindly by Dostoevsky in *The Diary of a Writer.* He became acquainted with Swedenborg, however, thanks to Aksakov's essays and translations, and he took from these books what suited his purpose.

### Swedenborg in the First Half of the Twentieth Century

During the first half of our century, much attention was paid to so-called symbolism in poetry. It seems strange that, in spite of this preoccupation, Swedenborg was little known. After all, Baudelaire's sonnet "Les Correspondances"—a poem crucial to symbolist poetics—took its title and its contents from Swedenborg. Curiosity alone should have directed critics to explore the original concept, not just its derivatives. The truth is that every epoch has dusty storage rooms of its own where disreputable relics of the past are preserved. Swedenborg was left there

together with the quacks, miracle workers, and clairvoy-
ants so typical of the not-so-reasonable Age of Reason—
people such as Count Cagliostro, the legendary Count
Saint-Germain, and an initiator of the "mystical lodges" in
France, Martinez Pasqualis. The risk of taking Swedenborg seriously was too great; besides, nobody seemed to
know what to think of him.

Neither his contemporaries nor posterity ought to be
blamed too much for this neglect. Swedenborg's destiny
was extraordinary. A scientist of wide reputation who pursued researches in various disciplines from geology to
anatomy, a member of the Royal Mining Commission in
Sweden, he had a sudden moment of illumination, abandoned his scientific pursuits, and produced a voluminous
oeuvre in which he described his travels through heaven
and hell and his conversations with spirits. He continued
to frequent the high society to which he belonged as a
royal counselor; and, even though he claimed to move simultaneously in the other world, his congeniality and
humor disarmed those who would have been ready to call
him a madman. After his death in 1772, his works, translated into English, made several converts who organized
themselves into the Swedenborgian Church of the New
Jerusalem. Romanticism in its turn made use of Swedenborg, adapting him to its own needs. For its adherents, an
ethereal, spiritual world opposed to the world of matter
was almost alluring: it was this they saw, albeit not quite
correctly, in Swedenborg's teachings. Balzac's Séraphita is
typical of such a romantic misinterpretation.

Swedenborg's legend was still alive at the time of Balzac
and Baudelaire, but gradually it waned during subsequent

decades. In the period that interests us, namely, the first half of the twentieth century, Swedenborg was at best an enigma attracting explorers of mental abnormality. It will suffice here to mention two major names that exemplify an attitude of uncertainty, if not of actual helplessness.

The first name is that of Karl Jaspers, who published a study of schizophrenia in 1922; he chose Strindberg, Van Gogh, Swedenborg, and Hölderlin as cases of famous schizophrenics. The second name is that of Paul Valéry, whose 1936 essay on Swedenborg is quite curious. Valéry was once at the center of the symbolist movement; moreover, as a brilliant essayist, he dominated the French literary scene for several decades. He confesses that Swedenborg has always been for him no more than a literary myth and leaves one wondering whether he has ever read the author with whom he is dealing. Valéry's essay was written as an introduction to the French translation of a book on Swedenborg by the Swedish scholar Martin Lamm. The book does not provide any answer to the question that preoccupies Valéry, namely: "How is a Swedenborg possible?" So, he looks for a solution of his own, rejecting the most common hypotheses, those of charlatanism and of insanity. But his own, psychological, explanation sounds even less convincing than Jaspers's diagnosis of mental illness and betrays Valéry's positivistic bias. His rather weak essay on Swedenborg offers us an insight into the positivistic background of French symbolism, into its basic duality. Swedenborg's visions were, according to Valéry, a kind of daydreaming—they occurred in a state between sleep and wakefulness. Perhaps we would not be guilty of insolence if we read into that statement, precisely because it lacks Valéry's usual sharpness, an avowal of his skepticism regarding creations of the human mind. He is very tactful and voices his respect for the "real" reality of nature and of human society; another reality, that of the artist, of the visionary, is autonomous, a separate area where veracity and delusion are on an equal footing.

Swedenborg was not the only writer who was something of a nuisance then. Another was William Blake. The question of Blake's mental illness was debated quite seriously at the beginning of our century; and, although his admirers rejected it as nonsense, their studies published in the 1930s and in the 1940s were known to relatively few people. The fact that Blake today has become a major figure of English literature is one of the signs indicating a serious change in attitude. And, of course, an acquaintance with Blake must awaken interest in Swedenborg, not only because Blake was influenced by him but also because Swedenborg can best be understood when approached using Blake's own criteria.

Let us pose a simplistic question: did Swedenborg really travel through heaven and hell, and did his conversations with spirits really take place? The most obvious answer is no, not really. He only believed that he had access to the other world at any time, for instance, when attending a party or walking in his garden. Everything happened only in his mind. This amounts to conceding that Jaspers was right when he pronounced his verdict: schizophrenia. We should note that romanticism had already treated Swedenborg in a way no different from the way positivistic psychiatry did later on, namely, a split into the material (that is, real) and the spiritual (that is, illusory) had been accepted, but with a plus sign, not a minus, added to the phantoms of our mind. If, however, William Blake's help is enlisted in reading Swedenborg, the picture changes radically. The question asked and the answer given would be rejected by Blake as absurd. Blake read Swedenborg exactly as he read Dante: these were for him works of the supreme human faculty, Imagination, thanks to which all men will one day be united in divine humanity. Through Imagination, spiritual truths are transformed into visible forms. While opposing Swedenborg on certain crucial matters, Blake felt much closer to his system than to the system of Dante, whom he accused of atheism. Blake's *The Marriage of Heaven and Hell* is modeled upon Swedenborg, and he would have been amused by an inquiry into whether he had "really" seen the devils and angels that he describes. The crux of the problem—and a serious challenge to the mind—is Blake's respect for both the imagination of Dante, who was a poet, and the imagination of Swedenborg, whose works are written in quite pedestrian Latin prose. Dante was regarded by his contemporaries as a man who had visited the other world. Yet Jaspers would not have called him a schizophrenic because the right of the poet to invent—that is, to lie—was recognized in Jaspers's lifetime as something obvious. It is not easy to grasp the consequences of the aesthetic theories that have emerged as the flotsam and jetsam of the scientific and technological revolution. The pressure of habit still forces us to exclaim: "Well, then, Swedenborg wrote fiction, and he was aware it was no more than fiction!" But, tempting as it is, the statement would be false. Neither Swedenborg nor Blake were aestheticians; they did not enclose the spiritual within the domain of art and poetry and oppose it to the material. At the risk of simplifying the issue by using a definition, let us say rather that they both were primarily concerned with the *energy* that reveals itself in a constant interaction of Imagination with the things perceived by our five senses.

## Swedenborgian Elements *in* Crime and Punishment

The doctrine of correspondences is treated at length in Swedenborg's *Heaven and Hell,* which Dostoevsky may have purchased or read in Aksakov's translation during his stay in Germany in 1865. Let us note the place of publication, Leipzig, and the date, 1863. *Crime and Punishment* was begun in Wiesbaden in 1865. That Baudelaire in his *Flowers of Evil* was indebted to Swedenborg is well known, but there are, in my opinion, strong traces of Swedenborg's influence in *Crime and Punishment* also. A big phantasmagoric city, whether it be Paris, literally called by Baudelaire *la cité infernale,* or St. Petersburg, where Raskolnikov is beset by nightmares, already seems to be the modern form of a Dantesque hell; a description of it may refer implicitly to the doctrine of correspondences. To sound convincing, one ought to quote numerous passages from Swedenborg. However, this is beyond the scope of a brief essay, and I shall limit myself to a few sentences. "What a correspondence is, is not known at the present day"—says Swedenborg—"for several reasons, the chief of which is that man has withdrawn himself from heaven by the love of self and love of the world" (*Heaven and Hell* 87). That lost vision embraced creation as a unity, because "the whole natural world corresponds to the spir-

FYODOR DOSTOEVSKY

itual world, and not merely the natural world in general, but also every particular of it; and, as a consequence, everything in the natural world that springs from the spiritual is called correspondent" (*Heaven and Hell* 89). Man by virtue of his mind is part of the spiritual world and, therefore, "whatever effects are produced in the body, whether in the face, in speech, or in bodily movements, are called correspondences" (*Heaven and Hell* 91).

Perhaps the gist of Swedenborg's teaching resides in his carrying the anthropocentric vision implied by Christianity to an extreme. The maxim "as above, so below" has always been invoked by hermetic Christian movements with their system of mirrors; for, according to them, the macrocosm was reflected in the microcosm, and thus correspondences are to be found in the whole tradition of alchemy and in Jakob Böhme. But Swedenborg went one step further: for him the whole universe in its only valid essence, celestial and spiritual or infernal, had a human shape: "It has been shown that the entire heaven reflects a single man, and that it is in image a man and is therefore called the Greatest Man" (*Heaven and Hell* 94). As a consequence, everything human acquires an extraordinary importance, for this entire world to which we apply physics and chemistry exists so as to provide *human* imagination with archetypes and human language with signs.[2] Any man may live in a constant relationship with the Greatest, Cosmic, Man—in other words, live in heaven—but he may also avoid it and keep company with the Cosmic Evil Man—in other words, live in hell. When he dies, he finds himself in one of the innumerable heavens or hells that are nothing other than societies composed of people of the same inclination. Every heaven or hell is a precise reproduction of the states of mind a given man experienced when on earth, and it appears accordingly—as beautiful gardens, groves, or the slums of a big city. Thus, everything on earth perceived by the five senses will accompany a man as a source of joy or of suffering much as the alphabet, once learned, may be composed into comforting or depressing books.

In the eighteenth century, Swedenborg was not alone in discovering this strange dimension: the dimension of human inwardness. Others as well searched for a counterbalance to the world of scientists, which was conceived as a mechanism seen *from the outside.* Different as they are from each other, in many ways several thinkers have in common this search for *the inside*: Berkeley with his *esse est percipi*—to be is to be perceived; Kant with his categories of the mind; and, of course, Blake. Swedenborg's choice of states of mind and images as the foundation of his system was to appeal to romantic and symbolist poets for obvious reasons. Yet, by shifting the emphasis, they obtained the opposite of the original idea. Correspondences are not symbols to be arbitrarily chosen by a poet or a novelist. If the word *symbol* applies here, they are "objective symbols," preordained by God and determined by the very structure of nature and of human imagination. A visionary, a prophet unveils them; and Swedenborg, who assigned himself a prophetic role, deciphered with their help the hidden spiritual meaning of the Bible. All this had little to do with literature, at least as far as he was concerned. It was not destined to become a basis for legitimizing uncontrolled subjectivity or for establishing a democratic equality of subjective symbols and metaphors. It is true that some poets have noticed that not all symbols are of equal power and they have valued the most those that have their roots in archetypes. But this is a separate issue, alien to Dostoevsky, at least on a conscious level.

In *Crime and Punishment*, the streets of St. Petersburg, the dust, the water of the canals, the stairs of tenement houses are described as seen by Raskolnikov; thus, they acquire the quality of his feverish states. His dreams, his coffinlike room, and the city itself are woven into the rich symbolic texture of the novel. All this is not unfamiliar to a reader of the early Dostoevsky and seems only to intensify the devices already used in *The Double* or in *The Landlady*. There is, however, one character who displays too much kinship with the spirits of Swedenborg for his direct descent from the book *Heaven and Hell* to be doubted. This is Svidrigailov. We will grant that he has captivated many readers and scholars who sensed in him a somewhat exotic element previously unencountered in Dostoevsky's novels. While a good deal of symbolism is involved in the name, appearance, and behavior of Sonya, we feel in Svidrigailov still another dimension, as though he had just arrived from and were returning to the beyond, in spite of his palpable presence and his presumed biography. Everything about him—the way he visits Raskolnikov for the first time, his physical features, his gestures, his speech, and his dreams—qualify as Swedenborgian correspondences; viewed from that angle, he is, though alive, a melancholy inhabitant of hell. In parenthesis, the strong identification of Dostoevsky with Svidrigailov has been noted by critics; but nobody, to my knowledge, has pointed to the origin of that hero's name to back the assumption. Dostoevsky was not indifferent to the past of his family, and he liked to refer to his ancestors, nobles who had owned an estate, Dostoevo, in the Grand Duchy of Lithuania. One of the Lithuanian rulers of the fifteenth century was Duke Svidrigaila, a well-known historical figure. No other character of Dostoevsky's is endowed with a Lithuanian name.

But unraveling the author's little secrets is more or less an idle game. What is important is that love of self, as a central theme, appears in *Crime and Punishment* in two forms: the one represented by Raskolnikov, who gradually becomes aware of its power; the other by his double, Svidrigailov, who has nothing to learn for he knows his evil nature and has a feeling of eternal damnation. Love of self, according to Swedenborg, characterizes all the inhabitants of the infernal realm, which remains, however, infinitely differentiated. To quote:

> Every evil, as well as every good, is of infinite variety
> That this is true is beyond the comprehension of those
> who have only a simple idea regarding every evil, such
> as contempt, enmity, hatred, revenge, deceit, and
> other like evils. But let them know that each one of
> these evils contains so many specific differences, and
> each of these again so many instances of particular dif-
> ferences, that a volume would not suffice to enumerate
> them. The hells are so distinctly arranged in accor-
> dance with the differences of every evil that nothing
> could be more perfectly ordered or more distinct. Evi-
> dently, then, the hells are innumerable.
>
> (*Heaven and Hell* 588)

Raskolnikov is an intellectual of the nineteenth century who has rejected heaven and hell as depicted in Christian iconography and rejected immortality along with them. The conversation between him and Svidrigailov on that subject is one of the strangest in world literature:

> "I don't believe in a future life," said Raskolnikov.
> Svidrigailov sat lost in thought.
> "And what if there are only spiders there, or some-
> thing of that sort," he said suddenly.

"He is a madman," thought Raskolnikov.

"We always imagine eternity as something beyond our conception, something vast, vast! But why must it be vast? Instead of all that, what if it's one little room, like a bathhouse in the country, black and grimy and spiders in every corner, and that's all eternity is? I sometimes fancy it like that."

"Can it be you can imagine nothing juster and more comforting than that?" Raskolnikov cried, with a feeling of anguish.

"Juster? And how can we tell, perhaps that is just, and do you know it's what I would certainly have made it," answered Svidrigailov, with a vague smile.

This horrible answer sent a cold chill through Raskolnikov.

How could we assume that this image of a private hell does not come straight from Swedenborg? Spiders, tarantulas, scorpions as symbols of evil return so persistently in Dostoevsky's late works that they deserve the appellation of correspondences. A passage from Swedenborg enlightens us sufficiently as to the hells that are built out of correspondences to things perceived by the senses:

Some hells present an appearance like the ruins of houses and cities after conflagrations, in which infernal spirits dwell and hide themselves. In the milder hells there is an appearance of rude huts, in some cases contiguous in the form of a city with lanes and streets, and within the houses are infernal spirits engaged in unceasing quarrels, enmities, fightings, and

brutalities; while in the streets and lanes robberies and
depredations are committed.

(Heaven and Hell 586)

Of course, in view of the infinite variety of hells, there is
room also for a country bathhouse with spiders.[3]

Svidrigailov suffers from the systematic visits of specters,
but he does not dismiss them as delusions. He is inclined
to think that "ghosts are, as it were, shreds and fragments
of other worlds, the beginning of them." The dreams he
has shortly before his suicide are so vivid that they resem-
ble visions more than sequences of blurred images loosely
bound together by an oneiric logic. Their horror sur-
passes even Raskolnikov's dream after the murder. One
would not be far wrong in considering *Crime and Punishment* a novel that deals with Raskolnikov's self-will on one
level only, while, on a deeper level, there is another crime
and another punishment: Svidrigailov's rape of a child
and his suicide. But is there any reason to think that
Svidrigailov had really committed that crime? Not necessarily. The coffin in which a fourteen-year-old girl lies
among flowers, like Shakespeare's Ophelia, may lead us to
believe that he had debauched an adolescent, who then
committed suicide. If so, he is a very sensitive devil indeed; for, in the next dream, the victim changes into a
five-year-old child, and he is terrified when suddenly she
opens her eyes and looks at him with "a glowing, shame-
less glance." Faced with Svidrigailov's presumed mis-
deeds, the reader is more or less in the position of
Dostoevsky's biographers, aware of his obsession and uncertain whether he had, in fact, once raped a little girl.

Just as in *Crime and Punishment*, the very core of evil had to do with the rape of a child, so in *The Possessed* Stavrogin, though he harbors in himself all the devils of Russia, accuses himself in his *Confession* of precisely the same sin. Yet his conversation with Tikhon leaves the reader perplexed. It is impossible to be certain that Stavrogin once behaved as he says he did. The purpose of his confession, reflected in the ugliness of its style, is noted by Tikhon: this is an act of defiance by Stavrogin, not of contrition; he does not ask for forgiveness but tries to provoke hatred and scorn. If this applies to the style, it may apply to the content as well, and the whole story of the rape might have been invented. It seems as if Dostoevsky's feelings of guilt were constantly searching for expression through one symbolic event that returns again and again as a fixed correspondence. That symbolic reality has the same substance as do Swedenborg's hells; it resides beyond commonly accepted notions of the existing and the imaginary, the objective and the subjective.

A literary parentage going back to Gogol and E. T. A. Hoffmann is sufficient to explain the fantastic elements in the young Dostoevsky's fiction, for instance, the pranks of Golyadkin Jr. in *The Double*, which are still explained away in a rational manner by Colyadkin Sr.'s mental illness. Beginning with *Crime and Punishment*, the rational cover for these extraordinary, bizarre occurrences grows very thin, and thus they are elevated above mere phantoms. A rational explanation is contrived in the form of a state between dreaming and wakefulness, as experienced by Svidrigailov on the night before his suicide; of a confession written by Stavrogin; of falling asleep in the *Dream of a Ridiculous Man*, though his travel through time into the remote past of mankind has nothing dreamy about it; or, in *The Brothers Karamazov*, of the sober, psychiatric title of a chapter: "The Devil. Ivan's Nightmare"—while neither Ivan nor the reader is convinced that the devil was merely a product of Ivan's sick brain.

## Dostoevsky as a Heresiarch

It is more than likely that Dostoevsky read Swedenborg when working on *Crime and Punishment* and that he was emboldened by a theology that assigns such a prominent place to the imagination. Whether and precisely what he borrowed from Swedenborg remains uncertain, with the possible exception of Svidrigailov's bathhouse full of spiders. But Dostoevsky's strategy as a religious thinker is of more consequence than possible borrowings of details, and Swedenborg's writings may offer some clues in this respect.

Anna Akhmatova used to call Dostoevsky and Tolstoy "heresiarchs," as we learn from Nadezhda Mandelstam's memoirs.[4] This is true enough. Their extraordinary minds, their fervor, and the gigantic stakes they played for did not save them from preaching fuzzy or even wild doctrines. Although basically dissimilar, they were alike in their efforts to adapt Christianity to what they believed to be the needs of modern man. Yet Tolstoy's "true" Christianity, diluted by Rousseauism, resembled more and more a nontheistic Buddhism, as Solovyov noted. In Tolstoy's copious output as a sermonizer, the metaphysical meaning of the Gospels evaporated and only the moral meaning remained. It would hardly be an exaggeration to

say that Tolstoy ended where Dostoevsky started and to lo-
cate the latter's point of departure during his Fourierist
phase, at the time when he belonged to the Petrashevsky
circle.

The Christian vocabulary of utopian socialism should
be kept in mind, whether its spokesman be Saint-Simon,
Fourier, or George Sand. In its rejection of Christian
churches and in placing itself under the sign of the
Gospels, utopian socialism was to some degree the inheri-
tor of such populist Christian movements of the past as
the Hussites or the Anabaptists, who had proclaimed a return to the original purity of the early Christian com-
munes. Yet the vocabulary veiled a profound change in
belief, a result of the eighteenth-century *Lumières*. A social
utopia now occupied the first place, not Christ: he was admired only as its announcer, as the most sublime teacher
and reformer. Dostoevsky, as we know, was shocked by Belinsky's derogatory and scornful words about Christ.
When he joined the Petrashevsky circle, it was different;
discussions on Fourier or Considérant did not threaten
his personal attachment to the figure of Jesus as a moral
ideal, for the precise reason that they focused upon the
Kingdom of God on earth as something not very remote
but easily attainable. Subsequently, Dostoevsky's whole
life, beginning with his stay in the penal colony of Omsk,
would be marked by the incessant struggle in his mind between two images of Christ: one, a model of perfection
never equaled by anyone else, yet still a mortal man and
thus subject to the law of death; the second, a God-Man
triumphant over death. A contradiction, overlooked by
the humanists and socialists of the Petrashevsky circle,

gradually was to take shape in Dostoevsky's work, up to its most poignant presentation in *The Legend of the Grand Inquisitor*. For the argument of the Grand Inquisitor with Christ is nothing more and nothing less than that of a utopian socialist with his supposed leader who refuses to serve as such and, what is worse, shows that his disciple had misunderstood him. Christ says, in fact, that his Kingdom of God is not of this world—and the freedom he offers man does not lead to any perfect society. No one but the God-Man intending to lift man up to his own divine level can ask for acceptance of this freedom. The utopian in Dostoevsky yearned so much for the Kingdom of God on earth that he sided with the Grand Inquisitor; it is this that explains the forceful speech the author, himself internally divided, puts into the mouth of his tragic old man. The divine nature of Christ appears as a major obstacle to human happiness on earth and, therefore, should be denied. But, by a dialectical countermovement, as soon as the earthly happiness of man is chosen as a goal, it becomes obvious that it can be attained only at the price of the total annihilation of human freedom. Thus, the argument expresses Dostoevsky's despair at the thought of the erosion of Christian faith—in himself, in the Russian intelligentsia, and in Western Europe. And it was this that forced him to resort to arbitrary and unrealistic remedies. In that big either/or—either a Christian civilization or the totalitarian society of Shigalev and of the Grand Inquisitor—he paradoxically hoped to find a third way and clung to his "Holy Russia" with the peasant below and the tsar above as the only possible mainstay of Christianity and, consequently, human freedom.

## The Human and the Divine

The problem of the two natures of Christ underlies Dostoevsky's whole work, and it also determines his journey from a socialist utopia to a nationalistic one. To say that at some given moment he became an atheist (whatever that word may mean) under Belinsky's influence is not truly relevant, for he was haunted by the figure of Christ the teacher perhaps no less in the 1840s than later on, when in the penal colony. Yet, undoubtedly, he underwent a change of heart in Omsk, in the sense that now the necessity of an act of faith became clear. His much-quoted letter of 1854 to Fonvizina, written upon his release from the prison camp, contains the nucleus of those internal contradictions that torment his major heroes:

> I will tell you regarding myself that I am a child of the age. that I have been a child of unbeliefs and doubt up till now and will be even (I know it) until my coffin closes. What terrific torments this thirst to believe has cost and still does cost me, becoming the stronger in my soul the more there is in me of contrary reasonings. And yet sometimes God sends me moments when I am utterly at peace; in those moments I have constructed for myself a symbol of faith in which everything is clear and sacred to me. This symbol is very simple: to believe that there is nothing more beautiful, more profound, more sympathetic, wiser, braver, or more perfect than Christ; and not only is there nothing, but, as I tell myself with jealous love, there could not be anything. Even more: if somebody proved to me that Christ is outside the truth, and if it were a fact that

> the truth excludes Christ, I would rather remain with
> Christ than with the truth.

This last sentence is potentially that of a "heresiarch."
Who could prove to Dostoevsky that Christ was beyond
the truth? A scientist, a philosopher, for whom everything
is submitted to deterministic laws and who would shrug at
the story of Christ rising from the dead as an offense to
our reason? That sort of proof, through the universal
order of nature, is accepted by those characters of Dostoevsky's who are, more or less, the spokesmen for his "intellectual part"—Ippolit in *The Idiot*, Kirillov in *The Possessed*,
and Ivan Karamazov. "And if Christ be not risen, then is
our preaching vain, and your faith is also vain," says Saint
Paul.[5] Ippolit, Kirillov, Ivan, and the Grand Inquisitor
have their negative proofs that it is really so; but they also
realize that, if it is so, if Christ deluded himself in foretelling his resurrection, then the world is a devil's farce.
Dostoevsky himself, or the part of him that turns against
his skeptical characters, "would rather remain with Christ
than with the truth" and thus yields the field in reality to
the so-called scientific *Weltanschauung*. The opposition of
faith to reason has behind it an old tradition, but the opposition of faith to truth is a desperate novelty and dan-
gerously favors any self-imposed deception.[6] There is
perhaps also a second layer of meaning in that enigmatic
sentence. Because the Gospels are not a treatise on ethics
and their message is often self-contradictory, many Christian mystics counseled clinging to the person of Christ as
opposed to norms or values. A well-founded counsel—but
at the same time a precept cherished by every sectarian,
for it authorizes transforming the image of Christ as suits

a given man or community. The suspicion arises whether "the Russian Christ" of Dostoevsky is not connected with such an exalted arbitrariness.

## The Onslaught of Philosophy—and of Gnosticism

A brief digression is necessary here. Christianity has in modern times, beginning with the Renaissance, been forced to renew its quarrel with philosophic thought. At one time, in the Roman empire, it had been Greek philosophy; assimilated and tamed by the church, it tended, nevertheless, to recover its autonomy; and at last—thanks to so-called humanism—it grew in strength, inspiring modern science. Or to be more precise, one side of Greek thought was now taken over and turned against the other, which had been fused with the Jewish heritage. Quite symptomatic was the revival in the sixteenth century of the Anti-Trinitarian heresy also known as Arianism, though Arius had been condemned by the Council of Nicaea long before, in A.D. 325. Perhaps one should call it *the* heresy and trace it down through the history of Christianity in its various contradictory guises. At first sight, the "luminous" rationalistic trend in the Renaissance (and, undoubtedly, Arianism, with its dislike of incomprehensible dogma, belongs here) had nothing to do with its contemporary "dark," more esoteric counterpart. Yet the two were just the two sides of the same philosophic coin, much as they had been before in the Hellenistic world. The origins of attacks upon the Trinity should be traced back to Gnosticism, which had already by the second century A.D. introduced a duality, a separation between Christ on the one hand and the God of the Old Testament on the other. The very dogma of the Trinity—of the three *hypostases* designated the Father, the Son, and the Holy Ghost—was elaborated as the response of the early church to that Gnostic cleavage that broke the continuity of the Revelation through history. From its birth, the Gnostic heresy, in its various ratiocinations, had at its core a resentment of the evil world: a God responsible for such evil could not be a supreme being, while Christ was—or represented— the true deity.[7] Then the Manichaeans stepped in and followed a well-blazed trail. Ever since, Christology has been a territory for which heretics have had a predilection; they have tended to oppose Redemption to Creation, the Savior to Jehovah, or even to exult in the human nature of Christ, who, through *kenosis*, "emptied himself" of his divine attributes. In Dostoevsky's major novels, all these problems are present implicitly or explicitly.

The theology of Swedenborg, who was both a modern Christian and a scientist, was a major attempt at wrestling with the dogma of the Trinity as recognized by all three branches of Christianity: Roman Catholic, Orthodox, and Protestant. He accused them all of teaching the faithful to imagine three gods and thus disguising polytheism under a formula incomprehensible to the human mind. At the same time, however, he disapproved of the solution offered by the Arians, for whom Christ was not of the same nature as the Father and for a large number of whom he was merely a man. Swedenborg's system is dominated by a

Christ who is *the only God*, not in spite of his having been born a man but precisely because he was born a man. Absolutely Christocentric, Swedenborg's system is also absolutely anthropocentric. Its most sacred books are the Gospel of Saint John and the Apocalypse; by coincidence, these were also the most sacred books for Dostoevsky. Swedenborg's credo is embodied in the exclamation of Thomas the Apostle when he touched Christ's wounds: "My Lord and my God." Man was created in the image and semblance of God, for Our Father in heaven is man; heaven, as I have already quoted, is, according to Swedenborg, the Greatest Man.

To compare Dante and Swedenborg as writers would be hazardous, but their respective visions of "the other shore" constitute two decisive testimonies to the imaginative life of our civilization. Dante's cosmology is medieval, and his theology is based upon Thomas Aquinas, in whose syllogisms Greek philosophy was put to a Catholic use. The importance of man, created and redeemed by God, is guaranteed in Dante by the Earth's central place in the universe. But by Swedenborg's time, the universe is resolved into a motion of whirling planets and stars. If it were not for one man, Christ, God incarnated, mankind would dwindle into a speck of dust, into an accident in the incomprehensible mechanical order of things. Perhaps for that reason Swedenborg emphasizes God—Man as preexisting, the Creator and Redeemer in one person. It would be incorrect to classify Swedenborg as an Anti-Trinitarian, for all he wanted was to propose a new concept of the Trinity. Yet his disciple William Blake, occasionally a rebel against his master, hardly modified the Swedenborgian doctrine when he chose the Human Form Divine as the key to all the secrets of existence. And, unlike in Swedenborg, gnostic affinities are obvious in Blake's multiple reversals of religious concepts: God the lawgiver equated with Satan, Elohim with inferior demiurges. The creation of the world, presented by Blake as an act of divine mercy *after* the Fall has already taken place (or simultaneously with it, which is the same where there is no time), is purely Manichaean. In the teachings of Mani (d. A.D. 277), the founder of Manichaeism, after the Kingdom of Light was contaminated by the Kingdom of Darkness, the Kingdom of Light allowed an inferior demiurge to create the world in that zone so that it might be purified through the action of time.

Swedenborg (and Blake) humanized or *hominized* God and the universe to such an extent that everything, from the smallest particle of matter to planets and stars, was given but one goal: to serve as a fount of signs for human language. Man's imagination, expressing itself through language and identical in its highest attainments with the Holy Ghost, was now to rule over and redeem all things by bringing about the era of the New Jerusalem. Man was again at the center, even though his Earth and his galaxy were not. The Christian strategy of Swedenborg (and Blake) perhaps parallels that of Thomas Aquinas, who felt that philosophy (or at least Aristotle, the philosopher) must be absorbed by Christian thought. In the eighteenth century, the Christian strategist was confronted with a more difficult task: philosophy was to be absorbed in its two derivatives, in the rationalistic trend and in the more somber heretical tradition of duality, of a chasm between

Creation and Redemption. It was made possible by affirming that the divine is eternally human and that the human is potentially divine.

But Swedenborg (and Blake) teetered on the very edge, where the equilibrium between Christian faith and its anti-Christian denial was constantly threatened. The divinization of man was already in the offing, accompanied by the advent of "European nihilism" as foretold by Friedrich Nietzsche. Our era, the second half of the twentieth century, is marked by a tragicomic escapism, namely, a "death of God" theology that proceeds from the idea of divine humanity and subjects it to an imperceptible alteration, so that it changes into its opposite. It is enough to read a book on Blake by one of the chief "death of God" theologians[8] to observe how this can be accomplished— obviously, by enlisting the help of Hegel. To Dostoevsky's credit, let us recall here that, while the dialectics of God-Man and Man-God were present in his novels, he desperately struggled against blurring the basic antinomy between the two.

### *Dostoevsky's Attempts to Solve the Problem*

When describing the books in Dostoevsky's library, Leonid Grossman admits the probability of Swedenborg's influence upon what we may consider Dostoevsky's last word in religious matters, namely, upon the discourses of Father Zosima on prayer, love, hell, and contact with other worlds. Grossman's hint has not, to my knowledge, been taken by anybody, and a study of the subject is lacking. Father Zosima in many of his pronouncements indeed sounds like Swedenborg, particularly in his talk on eternal damnation. A man's life, according to Zosima, is "a moment of *active living* love" and is given to him as a gift of time and space, where love can be exercised. The drama of eternal life resides precisely in the brevity of this encounter with time and space, which soon are no more, and then everything one has lived through becomes part of his interior states. The flames of hell are within the damned and correspond to the quality of their love on earth: "For them hell is voluntary and they cannot have enough of it. . . . They cannot behold the living God without hatred and demand that there be no God of life, that God destroy himself and all his creation."[9]

In Father Zosima's thinking, a Manichaean hatred of creation is characteristic of the damned. Yet Dostoevsky, like Swedenborg and Blake before him, tried hard to absorb the heresy and integrate it into a Christology of his own. In a novel, this is, however, more difficult than in theology and poetry. Dostoevsky seems to say: If the concept of God-Man free from sin is to have any validity, then human nature should allow us at least an inkling as to how it might be possible. That is why Dostoevsky spent so much energy striving to create a perfect good man as a hero of fiction. And he failed. Prince Myshkin is a living negative proof, for his acts show to what extent love of self is at the root of human nature and how insufficiently human someone is who lacks it. Myshkin, who is completely selfless, devoid of aggression and sexual drive is no less a monster of emptiness than is Stavrogin with his excess of self-love. Father Zosima comes straight from the lives of the saints and eludes our questioning, for he is protected by his prestige as a repentant sinner. As for Alyosha, he is convincing only as one of the Karamazovs, united by their dark, violent blood. His missionary activities among schoolboys and the resulting brotherhood are, to be frank, melodramatic and outright schmaltz. Artistic falsity reveals here the falsity of Dostoevsky's self-imposed collectivistic belief, his heresy that he propagated especially in his journalism. Alyosha, a Christlike leader, suggests the future Russian Christ and is surrounded by twelve children-disciples; but by a strange twist of stylistic fate (there are stylistic fates), the presumed church changes into a boy scout unit. It is a doubtful proposition that one can achieve the Kingdom of God on earth by converting mankind into boy scouts, and that is why those chapters of *The Brothers Karamazov* read like an unintended parody. Shatov in *The Possessed,* who loves the Christlike Russian people but does not believe in God, might, however, have been a sarcastic jab intentionally directed by Dostoevsky against himself.

In the history of the rebellion of man against God and against the order of nature, Swedenborg stands out as a healer who wanted to break the seals on the sacred books and thus make the rebellion unnecessary. By revealing that God is man, he was convinced that he had fulfilled Christ's promise to one day send a comforter, the spirit of truth; that spirit spoke through him. Swedenborg's serene Christology may help in elucidating Dostoevsky's tormented and tortuous Christology. At the same time, such a study would uncover some Blakean elements in Dostoevsky, who never heard of Blake.

Dostoevsky's rebels are invested with a false, exaggerated moral sensitivity: the order of the world should be rejected because it offends man's moral judgment; this world is full of the suffering and agony of creatures tormenting one another. The ideal man, Jesus, must stand in opposition to that natural order; unfortunately, he was for the rebels merely a man, and his mistakes had to be corrected: hence, the only logical conclusion was to postulate the advent of a Man-God. But Dostoevsky's "positive" heroes fare no better. His failures in drawing them probably testify to his utopian (Fourierist) vision of the ideal man as perfectly meek, perfectly humble, and deprived of selfhood. William Blake knew better: he distinguished between Imagination enslaved by the Spectre—by the self—and Imagination making use of the Spectre, which is a permanent component of human nature. Such an appraisal of human faculties is more realistic. But Dostoevsky's failures, even more than his successes, pay tribute to the permanence of the dilemma that, some eighteen centuries ago, emerged in the guise of a quarrel between the early Christian churches and the Gnostics. The divinization of man, when one abhors the order of the world as essentially evil, is a risky and self-contradictory venture.

## Notes

1. L. P. Grossman, *Seminarii po Dostoevskomu* (Seminar on Dostoevsky) (Gosudarstvennoe Izdatel'stvo, 1922; reprint, Great Britain: Prideaux Press, 1972).

2. In this respect, the English metaphysical poet Thomas Traherne is Swedenborg's predecessor, as, for instance, in the following stanza:

> This made me present evermore
> With whatsoere I saw.
> An object, if it were before
> My Ey, was by Dame Natures Law,
> Within my Soul. Her Store
> Was all at once within me: all her Treasures
> Were my imediat and Internal Pleasures,
> Substantial Joys, which did inform my Mind.

With all she wraught,
My Soul was fraught,
And evry Object in my Heart a Thought
Begot, or was: I could not tell,
Whether the Things did there
Themselves appear,
Which in my Spirit truly seemd to dwell;
Or whether my conforming Mind
Were not even all that therin shind.

From "My Spirit," in *The Poetical Works of Thomas Traherne* (New York: 1965).

3. In Swedenborg's system, there are no angels and devils except the saved and the damned humans. To this Dostoevsky refers in his notebook of 1875-76: "Are there devils? I could never imagine what satan's would be like. Job. Mephistopheles. Swedenborg: bad people . . . about Swedenborg." From *The Unpublished Dostoevsky,* ed. Carl R. Proffer (Ann Arbor, MI: Ardis, 1975), vol. 2.

4. Nadezhda Mandelstam, *Vtoraya kniga* (Second Book) (Paris: YMCA Press, 1972).

5. 1 Corinthians 15:14.

6. Here Dostoevsky comes close to Kierkegaard, but the dichotomy is resolved by Kierkegaard, who tips the scales in favor of "inwardness," "subjectivity," and thus identifies faith with truth: "The truth is precisely the venture which chooses an objective uncertainty with the passion of the infinite." "But the above definition of truth is an equivalent expression for faith." "Faith is precisely the contradiction between the infinite passion of the individual's inwardness and the objective uncertainty." From *Concluding Unscientific Postscript* (Princeton, NJ: Princeton University Press, 1971), p. 182. A saying of Meister Eckhart's may be recalled here: "If God were able to backslide from truth, I would fain cling to truth and let God go."

7. "The following may be noted as the main points in the Gnostic conception of the several parts of the *regula fidei*:

a) The difference between the supreme God and the creator of the world, and therewith the opposing of redemption and creation, and therefore the separation of the Mediator of revelation from the Mediator of creation.

b) The separation of the supreme God from the God of the Old Testament, and therewith the rejection of the Old Testament, or the assertion that the Old Testament contains no revelations of the supreme God, or at least only in certain parts.

c) The doctrine of the independence and eternity of matter.

d) The assertion that the present world sprang from a fall of man, or from an undertaking hostile to God, and is therefore the product of an evil or intermediate being.

e) The doctrine that evil is inherent in matter and therefore is a physical potence [*sic!*].

f) The assumption of Aeons, that is, real powers and heavenly persons in whom is unfolded the absoluteness of the Godhead.

g) The assertion that Christ revealed a God hitherto unknown."

From Adolph Harnack, *History of Dogma* (New York: Dover, 1961), vol. 1, pp. 257–259. Harnack also lists other points.

8. Thomas J. Altizer, *The New Apocalypse: The Radical Christian Vision of William Blake* (Ann Arbor, MI: University of Michigan Press, 1967).

9. Grossman.

WILLIAM BLAKE

# The Human
# Face of God*

## BY KATHLEEN RAINE

The poem by William Blake entitled "The Divine Image" comes from *Songs of Innocence,* a collection of poems written for children and published in 1789, when Blake was thirty-two years old. No one, of whatever place, time, or religion, could fail to understand and to assent to the simple directness of its message:

> To Mercy, Pity, Peace and Love
> All pray in their distress;
> And to these Virtues of delight
> Return their thankfulness.
>
> For Mercy, Pity, Peace, and Love
> Is God, our father dear,
> And Mercy, Pity, Peace, and Love,
> Is Man, his child and care.

*This essay was originally published in the Swedenborg Foundation's edition of *Blake and Swedenborg: Opposition Is True Friendship* (1985). Dr. Raine also has published a full-length study of Blake's *Job* engravings of 1823–1824 entitled *The Human Face of God,* which is unrelated to this essay.

For Mercy has a human heart,
Pity a human face,
And Love, the Human form divine,
And Peace, the human dress.

Then every man, of every clime,
That prays in his distress,
Prays to the human form divine,
Love, Mercy, Pity, Peace.

And all must love the human form,
In heathen, turk or jew;
Where Mercy, Love, & Pity dwell
There God is dwelling too.[1]

For all the apparent simplicity of this poem, the depth of its resonance leads us into deep eschatological mystery. At first sight, it might appear to be a simple statement of the Christian doctrine of the Incarnation, but there is much in the poem that might be unacceptable to the apostolic church, Catholic and Protestant alike; for Blake is not writing of the historical Jesus but of "the human form in heathen, turk or jew"—a comprehensive phrase that embraces all the races and religions of mankind without exception.

How did it come about that Blake was able to make, with such luminous simplicity, this affirmation, which goes far beyond any conventional declaration of faith in Jesus Christ? He was a mystic, to be sure, but mystics are of their time and place. He was a reader of the Bible; and, in the first chapter of Genesis, it is written that God said, "Let us make man in our image, after our likeness. . . . So God created man in his own image, in the image of God created he him."[2] But these words have been variously interpreted. According to the Gospel of St. John, the first-created man who was "in the beginning with God" "was made flesh and dwelt amongst us" in the person of Jesus Christ, but not otherwise. There have been certain mystics—Meister Eckhardt, for example—who have understood the mystery of the Incarnation in a more universal sense, but these have generally been frowned upon. At the end of the eighteenth century, Blake spoke openly of a realization that had hitherto been the secret knowledge of a few. He was—and knew himself to be—prophetically inspired, and "The Divine Image" is the quintessence of his prophetic message—that God is "in the form of a man" and that the Incarnation is not particular but universal. Such is the power and certainty of Blake's genius that in simple words he cuts through all theological tangles to the mysterious heart of the Christian revelation. When Jesus affirmed "I and the father are one" and "he who has seen me has seen the father," his words were deemed blasphemous and led to his condemnation. Blake's religion, as he constantly declared, is "the religion of Jesus" (by which he does not necessarily mean as taught by the Christian church) and under the guise of "poetic license" the radical, not to say revolutionary, content of his affirmation passes unnoticed. Such poems as "The Divine Image" win the assent of the heart before their doctrinal implications become apparent. "Knowledge is not by deduction, but Immediate by Perception or Sense at once. Christ addresses himself to the Man, not to his Reason."[3] In Blake's terms, Jesus, "the true man," is the Imagination present in all. That innate Imagination assents to Blake's words as being as self-evident as the light of day.

Yet these words embody the spirit of a new age, a new apprehension of the Christian revelation. But when, in *The Marriage of Heaven and Hell*, Blake wrote that "a new heaven is begun," he spoke not on his own authority but as a follower of Emanuel Swedenborg, as a member of the Swedenborgian Church of the New Jerusalem. Wonderful as are Blake's poems, his visionary paintings, his aphorisms, it is, in essence, the doctrines of Swedenborg that Blake's works embody and to which they lend poetry and eloquence. So, unawares, the teachings of Swedenborg's Church of the New Jerusalem have permeated the spiritual sensibility of the English nation, through Blake. Few of the ever-growing numbers who regard Blake as a prophet of the New Age are aware that the coherent and revolutionary interpretation of the Christian mysteries that underlies Blake's prophecies is that of Swedenborg.

The writings of Swedenborg, stilted and voluminous, written in Latin at a time when Latin was ceasing to be the common language of the learned, have nonetheless had a profound influence throughout Protestant Europe and beyond; Henry Corbin himself saw the seminal significance of Swedenborg, whom he went so far as to describe as "the Buddha of the West."[4] Swedenborg was by profession neither philosopher nor theologian but a man of science, assessor of minerals to the Swedish government. He spent much time in London, where he had a small but devoted following, and might even have been seen by Blake as a boy, for Swedenborg died in London in 1772 when

Blake was fifteen. Doubtless Swedenborg had predecessors in the millennial tradition, stemming from Joachim
of Flora; but we must accept Swedenborg's word that his
extraordinary prophetic insight came to him not by study
but by what he described as an "opening" of his consciousness, which revealed to him the inner worlds that he
calls the "heavens" and the "hells"; and which those who
follow the terminology introduced by Henry Corbin
would call the *mundus imaginalis*: worlds not in space but
in mankind's inner universe. In his visions, it was shown to
Swedenborg that a "new church" had been established in
the heavens, following a "Last Judgment" passed on the
apostolic church, which was to be superseded by the
"Church of the New Jerusalem," the last and perfect revelation of the nature of Jesus Christ as the "Divine Human
ity:" a mystery that had hitherto been imperfectly
understood but that was, in the New Church, to be fully
revealed in the epiphany of the "Divine Human." This
New Church, of which Swedenborg's writings are the
scriptures, is to be the last in the 6,000 years of the world's
history from the creation to the end of days and the coming of the kingdom. There have already been, according
to Swedenborg, twenty-six such churches, from the time
of Adam, through a succession of prophetic revelations
made to the patriarchs, to Noah, Abraham, Moses, and
Solomon; and within the Christian era, the churches of
Paul, Constantine, Charlemagne, and Luther, each of
these representing some new realization—or revelation—
that is to reach its term and perfect fulfillment in a total
affirmation of the humanity of God and the divinity of
man, their unity and identity. In his setting out of the

leading doctrines of the Church of the New Jerusalem, Swedenborg declares that "the Lord is God from eternity" and that the Divine Human is not merely the Son of God but God himself. "God and man, in the Lord . . . are not two, but one person, yea, altogether one . . . He is the God of heaven and earth." The Divine Humanity is almighty; or, as Blake simply says, "God is Jesus" (LAOC; K 777). Since, in this teaching, the oneness of the human and the divine is total, it follows that the Christian revelation can go no farther, man and God being one, not only in the historic person of Jesus Christ but totally for the Christ within the whole human race.

Carl Jung has written in criticism of the Christian church that—if not in principle, at all events in practice—the Divine Being has been envisaged as outside man and the Redemption (in the doctrine of the Atonement) also as an occurrence outside man, occurring once only in history. It is true that the mass is held to be not a commemoration of that event but a timeless reenactment; but even so, that mystery, as commonly taught and understood, is an external and historical event. Jesus Christ, moreover, is an exceptional being, virtually a demigod in the pagan sense, not fully human. Jung, in his remarkable work *Answer to Job*, admired by Henry Corbin[5] and expressing the mature thought of a lifetime on the meaning of Christianity, writes that

> Christ, by his descent, conception and birth, is a half-god in the classical sense. He is virginally begotten by the Holy Ghost and, as he is not a creaturely human being, has no inclination to sin. The infection of evil was in his case precluded by the preparations for the

Incarnation. He therefore stands more on the divine
than on the human level.[6]

The same is true of the Virgin Mary: "As a consequence of
her immaculate conception Mary is already different
from other mortals, and this fact is confirmed by her assumption."[7] Thus, salvation is available to humankind
through the external intervention of these superhuman
personages. In making this criticism of Christianity, Jung
makes no mention of Swedenborg's teachings (he had, in
fact, read Swedenborg early in his life), which did raise
and respond to many of his own criticisms, in calling for
an interiorization of the Christian mysteries of the Incarnation, Passion, and Resurrection. Swedenborg gives an
actual date—1757 (which was, incidentally, the date of
Blake's birth)—when a "Last Judgment" had been passed
on the apostolic church "in the heavens"—that is to say, in
mankind's inner worlds—to be followed by an epiphany
of the Divine Humanity in his full glory in the inner
worlds or "heavens." With this inner event, a new kind of
realization, a new kind of consciousness, began to dawn
within Christendom, following the interiorization of the
apostolic teaching. This Last Judgment was not an outer
event, in time and in history, but an inner event, which
would, not dramatically but gradually, make itself apparent also in the outer world of history. A new church is,
thus, a new consciousness. Without invoking the idea of
"evolution" (as understood by materialist science), we are
to understand Swedenborg's concept of the twenty-seven
churches as a progressive revelation in time and history.
This is entirely in keeping with the linear view of time
common to all the Abrahamic religions (Judaism,

Christianity, and Islam); and, indeed, without such a conception time and history become meaningless. Blake saw the twenty-seven churches as cyclic rather than linear, a progressive darkening of the paradisal vision from Adam to Jesus Christ, followed by a progressive recovery to be fulfilled in the "second coming" in the inner worlds. This event completes the cycle that leads humankind back to the paradisal state from which we have fallen.

What is under consideration is not in its nature an event to be pinned down like an event in history to a certain date but is rather a subtle change of awareness. It seems that such a change in the understanding of the nature of spiritual events did begin to manifest itself at that time, which has continued to grow like a plant from a small seed. Swedenborg's seed fell on fertile ground in the spirit of William Blake. It may well be that in the future our own time will be seen not as the age of the triumph of materialist science but as the breakdown of that phase and the beginning of just such an "opening" of humanity's inner worlds as Swedenborg prophetically experienced and foresaw.

This theme is a central one for Jung, who, in his *Answer to Job*, sets forth at length a view of the Bible in which, from Job to the Incarnation of Jesus Christ, there is what he calls "a tendency for God to become man." This tendency is already implicit in Genesis, when, by a special act of creation, Jahweh created man, who was the image of God. Jung is, of course, using the terms not of theology but of psychology and is, therefore, writing of changes in human consciousness of the Divine Being and not of changes in God himself in an absolute sense. Jung writes:

In omniscience, there had existed from all eternity a
knowledge of the human nature of God or of the divine nature of man. That is why, long before Genesis
was written, we find corresponding testimonies in ancient Egyptian records. Preparations, however, are not
in themselves creative events, but only stages in the
process of becoming conscious. It was only quite late
that we realized (or rather, are beginning to realize)
that God is Reality itself and therefore—last but not
least—man. This realization is a millennial process.[8]

Jung sees this process foreshadowed in the story of
Job—the type of the human encounter with the Divine.
The God of the Book of Job is so totally other that Job
seems to himself to be insignificant, powerless, without recourse—except to God himself; and Jung is in agreement
with theologians who have seen in Job's words, "I know
that my redeemer liveth, and that he shall stand in the latter day upon the earth . . . yet in my flesh shall I see
God,"[9] a foreshadowing of the Incarnation:

The life of Christ is just what it had to be if it is the life
of a god and a man at the same time. It is a *symbolus*, a
bringing together of heterogenous natures, rather as if
Job and Yahweh were combined in a single personality.
Yahweh's intention to become man, which resulted
from his collision with Job, is fulfilled in Christ's life
and suffering.[10]

On the way to this realization, Jung points out, we have
Ezekiel's vision of the "Son of Man," which reappears in
the Book of Daniel, and later (about 100 B.C.) in the

Book of Enoch. Ezekiel is himself addressed as "Son of Man"—the man on the throne whom he beheld in his vision and, hence, a prefiguration of the much later revelation in Christ. Daniel had a vision of the "Ancient of Days," to whom "with the clouds of heaven there came one like the son of man." Here the "son of man" is no longer the prophet himself but a son of the "Ancient of Days" in his own right.

I suggest that the power of Swedenborg's revelation and of Blake's prophetic writings lies in the reality of what they describe, a growing inner awareness on which we cannot go back. Jung and even Freud were aware of this process of interiorization of the mysteries, but they were not the first to challenge the externalized consciousness of post-Cartesian science; "The Divine is not in Space," Swedenborg affirmed, "although the Divine is omnipresent with every man in this world, and with every angel in heaven" (*Divine Love and Wisdom* 7). This, it may be said, has always been so and is implicit in every religious tradition; yet as a fact of the history of 2,000 years of Christendom, the realization has been progressive and come but slowly. Seen in another way, Swedenborg's teaching can be seen as a return to a lost traditional norm at the height of the age of Deism or "natural religion" as a philosophic creed, whose effects in every sphere of life are still dominant in our own world. Materialist science has identified "reality" as the natural order, conceived to be an autonomous mechanism external to mind; in his denial of this view of the "real," Swedenborg, it might be said—and Blake no less—restored a lost norm that understands that mind is not in space but space in mind.

The Divine (Swedenborg declared) is everywhere, yet not in space; and he insists that

> these things cannot be comprehended by a natural
> idea because there is space in that idea; for it is formed
> out of such things as are in the world; and in each and
> all these things, which strike the eye, there is space.
> Everything great and small is of space; everything,
> broad and high there is of space; in short every mea-
> sure, figure and form there is of space.
>
> (*Divine Love and Wisdom* 7)

Swedenborg strove to remove the identification of reality with an external material order. Space is a function of the natural body, but the human spirit is capable of the omnipresence of the nonspatial.

Furthermore, it is not God who is omnipresent spirit while man exists in space; because "God is Very Man" (*Divine Love and Wisdom* 289), the human universe is likewise boundless spirit, as God is. Swedenborg writes:

> In all the heavens there is no other idea of God than
> the idea of a man; the reason is, that heaven as a
> whole, and in every part is in form as a man and the
> Divine, which is with the angels, constitutes heaven;
> and thought proceeds according to the form of
> heaven; wherefore it is impossible for the angels to
> think of God otherwise. Hence it is that all those in the
> world who are conjoined with heaven (that is with the
> inner worlds) when they think interiorly in themselves,
> that is, in their spirit, think of God in a like manner.

For this cause that God is a Man. . . . The form of
heaven affects this, which in its greatest and in its least
things is like itself.

(Divine Love and Wisdom 11)

Heaven in its whole and in every part is "in form as a
man"; and because man was created "after the image and
likeness of God," "the ancients, from the wise to the simple"—from Abraham to the primitive Africans—thought
of God as a man. This is not anthropomorphism in the
sense in which the word is currently understood, as a pro-
jection of the human image upon the divine mystery, but
rather the reverse: a recognition of the divine image imprinted on the inner nature of humankind, as "the Divine
Human," to use Swedenborg's term. "All is Human,
Mighty, Divine," Blake writes and summarizes the Swedenborgian teaching in a quatrain:

> God Appears & God is Light
> To those poor Souls who dwell in Night,
> But does a Human Form Display
> To those who dwell in Realms of day.
>
> (AI; K 434)

These lines are the reversal of the "enlightened" view that
we cease to see God in human form as we learn more
about "the universe" as natural fact. The ultimate knowledge, according to Blake and Swedenborg, is that the universe is contained in mind—a view to be found also in the
Gnostic writings, in the Vedas, and in other spiritually profound cosmologies of the East, but long forgotten in the
West with its preoccupation with externality. Thus, we are
given a conception of humanity totally other than that of a

materialist science: man in his spiritual being is boundless and contains not a part of his universe but its wholeness and infinitude. The "body" of the Divine Human is not contained in natural space but contains all things in itself. Swedenborg writes, "His human body cannot be thought of as great or small, or of any stature, because this also attributes space; and hence He is the same in the first things as the last and in the greatest things and the least; and moreover the Human is the innermost of every created thing, but apart from space" (*Divine Love and Wisdom* 285).

Swedenborg uses a strange but cogent argument for the humanity of the Divine: that the attributes of God would be inconceivable except in human terms; and since God is knowable only in human terms, God must, therefore, possess human attributes:

> That God could not have created the universe and all
> things thereof, unless He were a Man, may be very
> clearly comprehended by an intelligent person from
> this ground that . . . in God there is love and wisdom,
> there is mercy and clemency, and also there is absolute
> Goodness and Truth, because these things are from
> Him. And because he cannot deny these things, nei-
> ther can he deny that God is a Man: for not one of
> these things is possible abstracted from man: man is
> their subject, and to separate them from their subject
> is to say that they are not. Think of wisdom and place it
> outside man. Is there anything? . . . It must be wisdom
> in a form such as man has, it must be in all his form,
> not one thing can be wanting for wisdom to be in it. In
> a word, the form of wisdom is a man; and because man
> is the form of wisdom, he is also the form of love,

mercy, clemency, good, and truth, because these make
one with wisdom.

(*Divine Love and Wisdom* 286)

It is for these reasons, Swedenborg argues, that humanity
is said to be created in the image of God, that is, into the
form of love and wisdom. It cannot be that mankind invented God in its own image, since that image is already
imprinted in us in our very being. The argument is a subtle one; and although it could be asked whether God
could not have created universes and beings other than
man, the same argument would in every case apply: whatever their attributes, these too would bear the image and
imprint of their creator and source. Blake—who had read
and annotated Swedenborg's *Divine Love and Wisdom* with
evident delight—might, when he wrote his poem "To
Mercy, Pity, Peace and Love," have been thinking of this
very passage.

Swedenborg dismisses the idea of those who think of
God as other than as a man, and "of the divine attributes
otherwise than as God as a man, because, separated from
man, they are figments of the mind. God is very Man,
from whom every Man is a man according to his recep-
tion of love and wisdom" (*Divine Love and Wisdom* 289).

So it is that:

> . . . Mercy has the human heart,
> Pity a human face,
> And Love, the human form divine,
> And Peace, the human dress.

"The human form divine" is not the natural body idola-
trously glorified, but the spiritual form of our human
nature.

In understanding that, when he wrote these words, so luminously simple, Blake is propounding Swedenborgian doctrine, it becomes perfectly clear that no humanism is implicit in his assigning the human attributes to God, the source and author of our humanity. Swedenborg wrote that, "*in all forms and uses there is a certain image of man,*" and that "all uses from primes to ultimates to primes, have relation to all things of man and correspondences with him, and therefore man in a certain image is a universe; and conversely the universe viewed as to its uses is man in an image" (*Divine Love and Wisdom* 317). Swedenborg draws the conclusion that it is for this reason that man is called a microcosm, since the universe is totally present in all its parts. Or again, in Blake's words, "One thought fills immensity." What Swedenborg is saying in his stilted style—and Blake is repeating in what to his contemporaries seemed "wild" poetic ravings—is, in fact, of extreme subtlety and great profundity: that human consciousness contains its universe. This is a return to the ancient teaching, as found, for example, in the *Hermetica,* that mind is not in space, but all spaces and whatever these contain, in mind: "Nothing is more capacious than the incorporeal." To have reaffirmed this realization in the eighteenth century attests to an insight so extraordinary that it can only be described—and Swedenborg did so describe it—as a prophetic revelation.

But if for Swedenborg the true man is not the natural body, he, nevertheless, insists in great detail on the minutiae of the spiritual anatomy:

> Because God is a Man, He has a body, and everything belonging to the body; consequently He has a face, a breast, an abdomen, loins, feet; for apart from these he

would not be a Man. And having these, He has also
eyes, ears, nostrils, mouth, tongue, and further the or-
gans that are within a man, as the heart and lungs, and
the parts which depend on these . . . but in God Man
they are Infinite.

(*Divine Love and Wisdom* 21)

He insists "that the angelic spirits are in every respect
human . . . they have faces, eyes, ears, hearts, arms, heads
and feet; they see, hear and converse with one another
and, in a word, that no external attribute of man is want-
ing, except the material body" (*Heaven and Hell* 75). In describing realities of the imaginal world, Swedenborg insists
on the clarity and distinctness of the spirits: "I have seen
them in their own light, which exceeds by many degrees
the light of the world, and in that light I have observed all
parts of their faces more distinctly and clearly then ever I
did the faces of men on earth" (*Heaven and Hell* 75).

It is hard to know whether Blake possessed this faculty
or if he is paraphrasing Swedenborg, so closely do their
accounts tally:

A Spirit and a Vision are not, as the modern philosophy supposes, a cloudy vapour, or a nothing: they are
organized and minutely articulated beyond all that the
mortal and perishing nature can produce. He who
does not imagine in stronger and better lineaments,
and in stronger and better light than his perishing,
and mortal eye can see, does not imagine at all. The
painter of this work asserts that all his imaginations appear to him infinitely more perfect and more minutely

organized than any thing seen by his mortal eye. Spirits are organized men.

(DC; K 576–577)

This is pure Swedenborg; but it may be that we also have
to conclude that those gifted with the clear vision of the
imaginal world are in essential agreement because describing the same reality.

To return to Swedenborg, he affirms continually that the
universal heaven is in the form of a man, and "each society
in heaven, be it large or small, is so likewise; hence also an
angel is a man, for an angel is heaven in its least form"
(*Heaven and Hell* 52, 53). Thus, every part down to the smallest "heaven in its least form" is infinite and the Divine
Human, an infinite whole made up of infinite wholes; and
"the universal heaven consists of myriads of myriads of angels" (*Divine Providence* 63). (Here, it must be said that
Swedenborg's angels are also men but discarnate. The word
*angel,* as he uses it, is not to be understood in the sense of
the Near Eastern religions, or indeed of the Christian fathers and Dionysius the Areopagite's celestial hierarchies.)

The human form is present throughout the universe
alike in its greatest and in its least parts. Swedenborg
writes that "in God Man infinite things are distinctly one.
It is well known that God is Infinite, for he is called the Infinite. He is not infinite by this alone, that He is very *Esse*
and *Existere* in Himself, but because there are Infinite
things in Him" (*Divine Love and Wisdom* 17). The "vision
of light" Blake described in a letter to a friend is purely
Swedenborgian; every infinitesimal part of nature is
human—and this is his answer to Newton's theory that
light is made of "particles":

In particles bright
The jewels of Light
Distinct shown & clear.
Amaz'd & in fear
I each particle gazed,
Astonish'd, Amazed;
For each was a Man
Human-form'd. Swift I ran,
For they beckon'd to me
Remote by the Sea,
Saying: Each grain of Sand,
Every Stone on the Land,
Each rock & each hill,
Each fountain & rill,
Each herb & each tree,
Mountain, hill, earth & sea,
Cloud, Meteor & Star,
Are Men Seen Afar.[11]

Swedenborg's Grand Man of the Heavens is a concept of great splendor. In this Divine Man or Human Divine, all lives are contained, individually and as angelic societies within the one life of the Divine Humanity; and so down to every inhabitant of heaven who is "every one in his own heaven" and the whole is reflected in each. "The Lord leads all in the universal heaven as if they were one angel" and in the same way "an angelic society sometimes appears as one man in the form of an angel" (*Heaven and Hell* 51), So "when the Lord himself appears in the midst of the angels, he does not appear encompassed by a multitude but as one in an angelic form" (*Heaven and Hell* 52). "I have seen," Swedenborg writes of a visionary society, that "when at a distance it appears as one, and on its approach, as a multitude" (*Heaven and Hell* 62). And again it is hard to know whether Blake is describing his own vision or paraphrasing Swedenborg when he writes: "The various States I have seen in my imagination; when distant they appear as One Man but as you approach they appear multitudes of nations" (VLJ; K 609). Blake summarizes the essence of the Swedenborgian vision of the Grand Man in a passage several times repeated in the Prophetic Books:

> Then those in Great Eternity met in the Council of
>   God
> As one man. . . .
>
> As one Man of all the Universal Family; & that One Man
> They call Jesus the Christ, & they in him & he in them
> Live in Perfect harmony, in Eden the land of life.
>
> (FZ; K 277)

Eden, the land of life, is the *Mundus imaginalis*, the "bosom of God,"—our native place and state.

In affirming the humanity of God, Swedenborg is, nevertheless, remote from what is now called "humanism"; for man is (in Blake's words) only "a form and organ of life" and the life of every individual, or every community, of the whole creation, is "from the Lord." No man's life belongs to himself, each is a recipient of the one life. Thus, whereas Blake wrote that "God is Man & exists in us & we in him,"[12] this is no more nor less than the teaching of St. John's Gospel and the words of Jesus, "as thou, Father, art in me, and I in thee, that they also may be one in us."[13] Created beings and men exist by virtue of what Swedenborg calls the "influx" of the one divine life. This influx is through the inner worlds; the outer world of natural appearances is the mirror of spiritual realities but has itself no substance. (This is, of course, the teaching of Plotinus on nature and of other Platonic writers.) But the outer form—whether of human being or animal, plant, or mineral—is the "correspondence" of their living nature. Nothing in nature is, as for materialist science, a self-existent physical entity subject to natural causes; indeed, for Swedenborg there is no such thing as a natural cause, all causes being spiritual and "nature," the lowest effect. Again, Blake is giving expression to this doctrine when he writes that "every Natural Effect has a Spiritual Cause, and Not a Natural; for a Natural Cause only seems: it is a Delusion of Ulro & a ratio of the perishing Vegetable Memory" (M 27; K 513). The realities mirrored in nature belong to the imaginal world—in Blake's terms, the Imagination.

> This world of Imagination is the world of Eternity; it is the divine bosom into which we shall all go after the death of the Vegetated body. This World of Imagination is Infinite and Eternal, whereas the world of Generation, or Vegetation, is Finite & Temporal. There Exist in that Eternal World the Permanent Realities of Every Thing which we see reflected in this Vegetable Glass of Nature. All Things are comprehended in their Eternal Forms in the divine body of the Saviour, the True Vine of Eternity, the Human Imagination.
>
> (VLJ; K 605–606)

Blake insists that the imaginal world is a plenitude of forms and, in the same work, writes:

> Many suppose that before the Creation All was Solitude & Chaos. This is the most pernicious Idea that

can enter the Mind, as it . . . Limits All Existence to
Creation & to Chaos, to the Time & Space fixed by the
Corporeal Vegetative Eye . . . Eternity Exists & all
things in Eternity, Independent of Creation.

(VLJ; K 614)

While Blake's account of the imaginal world bears a
more Platonic stamp than does Swedenborg's, with
Blake's emphasis on the inner forms of the Imagination
as the originals of which the natural forms are images or
copies, yet it is evident that Swedenborg's accounts of
heavenly scenery are describing the same imaginal reality.
The destination of the discarnate soul is not an empty nir-
vana but comparable to the Far Eastern paradises that
await the discarnate soul after death and the similar paradises and hells of the Near and Middle Eastern religions.
In *Divine Love and Wisdom* (321), Swedenborg writes:

> The spiritual world in external appearance is quite
> similar to the natural world. Lands appear there,
> mountains, hills, valleys, planes, fields, lakes, rivers,
> springs of water, as in the natural world. . . . Paradises
> also appear there, gardens, groves, woods, and in them
> trees and shrubs of all kinds bearing fruit and seeds;
> also plants, flowers, herbs and grasses. . . . Animals ap-
> pear there, birds and fish of every kind.

Thus, in his systematic manner, Swedenborg spells out the
presence in the "heavens" of the mineral, vegetable, and
animal kingdoms. In Swedenborg's "heavens" and Blake's
Imagination, which both call the Divine Human [in Latin,
*Homo Maximus*], the whole universe is contained in its infinite variety as the diversification of the single being of
the Divine Humanity. In an early work, *Vala,* or *The Four*

*Zoas*, Blake describes the whole natural creation striving—"groaning and travailing," in the words of St. Paul[14] to bring forth the human:

> . . . Man looks out in tree & herb & fish & bird & beast
> Collecting up the scatter'd portions of his immortal
>      body
> Into the Elemental forms of every thing that grows.
> . . . .
> In pain he sighs, in pain he labours in his universe
> Screaming in birds over the deep, & howling in the
>      wolf
> Over the slain, & moaning in the cattle & in the winds
> . . . .
> And in the cries of birth & in the groans of death his
>      voice
> Is heard throughout the Universe: wherever a grass
>      grows
> Or a leaf buds, The Eternal Man is seen, is heard, is felt
> And all his sorrows, till he reassumes his ancient bliss.
>
> (FZ; K 355)

Humanity, the immortal body "distributed," as the Platonist would say, in the "many," must be reassumed into the "one," the bosom of God, the human Imagination. In that universe, microcosm and macrocosm are one.

I mentioned earlier C. G. Jung's highly significant criticisms of the Christian church for its conversion of the figures of Jesus Christ, and in the Catholic church the Virgin Mary likewise, into what have been to all intents and purposes pagan demigods. Jung's criticisms of Christianity have indeed been cogent, and he has played a significant part in calling for an interiorization of the Christian mysteries. In the introduction to his work on *Psychology and Alchemy,* he writes:

> We can accuse Christianity of arrested development if we are determined to excuse our own shortcomings. In speaking therefore not of the deepest and best understanding of Christianity but of the superficialities and disastrous misunderstandings that are plain to see. The demand made by the *imitatio Christi*—that we should follow the ideal and seek to become like it—ought logically to have the result of developing and exalting the inner man. In actual fact, however, the ideal has been turned into an external object of worship, and it is precisely this veneration for the object that prevents it from reaching down into the depths of the soul and transforming it into a wholeness in keeping with the ideal. Accordingly the divine mediator stands outside as an image, while man remains fragmentary and untouched in the deepest part of him.[15]

—and later in the same work:

> It may easily happen, therefore, that a Christian who believes in all the sacred figures is still undeveloped and unchanged in his innermost soul because be has "all God outside" and does not experience him in the soul. . . . Yes, everything is to be found outside—in image and in word, in Church and Bible—but never inside. . . . Too few people have experienced the divine image as the innermost possession of their own souls. Christ only meets them from without, never from within the soul.[16]

This summons to our time to discover the God within may be seen as perhaps Jung's greatest contribution—and a very great one it is. But Jung seems not to have been aware of Swedenborg as a predecessor and prophet of just such a transformation of consciousness as he himself wished to see. Swedenborg, on his part, would have seen Jung as one fulfillment of his prophecy, his vision of a Last Judgment in the heavens passed on the apostolic church, to be followed by the appearance of the Lord in the inner heavens. Jung writes of the "God-image," the divine signature or archetype, imprinted in every soul. Accused by theologians of "psychologism" for making his appeal to this God-image (whose presence is testified, nevertheless, in the first chapter of Genesis) and thereby of "deifying the soul," Jung replied, "When I say as a psychologist that God is an archetype, I mean by that the 'type' in the psyche. The word 'type' is, as we know, derived from τυποσ 'blow' or 'imprint'; thus, an archetype presupposes an imprinter."[17] The argument is very close to that of Swedenborg, that human qualities must mirror divine qualities. In this respect, Henry Corbin, in the review already cited, defends Jung, he himself being deeply concerned with defining and discovering the "imaginal" world.

> True, C.G. Jung chooses not to speak otherwise than
> as a psychologist, and deals only with psychology; he
> does not claim to be a theologian or even a philoso-
> pher of religion. But having said "Only a psychologist,
> only psychology" one has the sudden sense of having
> committed a grave injustice, of associating oneself by
> that way of speaking with all those who, mistrusting for
> one reason or another the implications of Jung's

works, close the matter after each one with the comment "it is *nothing but* psychology." But one may well
ask oneself what they have done with their *soul*, with
their *Psyche* to dismiss it in this way and to dare to
speak of it in terms of being "nothing but that." So why
when one has shown that there are psychological fac-
tors which correspond to divine figures, do some people find it necessary to cry blasphemy as if all were lost
and those figures devaluated?[18]

Swedenborg too had insisted that the imprint of the infinite and eternal is within every form and, moreover, that
the infinite and eternal is present in the infinite variety of
things, "in that no substance, state or thing in the created
universe can ever be the same or identical with any other."
So that in none of the things that fill the universe can any
sameness be produced to all eternity. This (he continues)
is perspicuously evident in the variety of faces of all
human beings; "not one face exists in the whole world
which is the same as another, neither can exist in all eternity; nor therefore one mind for the face is the type of the
mind" (*Divine Love and Wisdom* 315). Here Swedenborg is
using the word *type*—imprint—in exactly Jung's sense. Yet,
by influx, all these are forms of the divine image, in
Blake's words:

> . . . the Divine—
> Humanity who is the Only General and Universal
> Form
> To which all Lineaments tend & seek with love &
> sympathy.
>
> ( J; K 672)

There is not one image or face of God but an infinity of images, an infinity of faces. The implications are overwhelming, for it follows that every human face in the world is, insofar as it is open to the divine influx, one of the myriad faces of God. Was it not this mystery that Jesus himself sought to impart in the parable that tells how the "Son of Man" says to the Just, "I was an hungered and ye gave me meat, I was thirsty and ye gave me drink; I was a stranger and ye took me in, naked and ye clothed me: I was in prison and ye came unto me."[19] The Just ask,

> Lord, when saw we thee an hungered, and fed thee?
> Or thirsty and we gave thee drink? When saw we thee a
> stranger and took thee in? Or naked, and clothed
> thee? . . . and the King shall answer and say unto them
> . . . inasmuch as ye have done it unto one of the least
> of these my brethren, ye have done it unto me.[20]

and so with the Unjust, who have rejected in all these the "Son of Man." Whereas the conventional reading may be that to serve the hungry and thirsty, strangers and prisoners, is equivalent to serving the Lord in person, the plain reading of the text is that it actually is the Divine Humanity who is present in all these.

Swedenborg claimed for his Church of the New Jerusalem that it is to be the ultimate Christian revelation and understanding of the Son of God in his Divine Humanity—and indeed it is not possible to conceive a closer union of God and Man than in this universal influx of divinity in all creation and in all humankind.

To turn once again to Jung's remarkable diagnosis of our present situation, *Answer to Job*: He describes the gradual emergence, in the Bible, of the idea of God as man, becoming ever clearer from Job to Ezekiel to Daniel, to the Book of Enoch, and finally to the Incarnation of Jesus Christ. But Jung, like Swedenborg, does not see the gradual realization as ending there. As Swedenborg in the symbol of his twenty-seven churches sees, from the time of Jesus, not one but several successive churches emerging and falling into decay, so does Jung see the Christian Revelation as incomplete. As a psychologist, he had witnessed, over a long lifetime, the pressure within the human soul itself toward some further understanding. Whereas Swedenborg saw the awaited completion as a perfected understanding of the nature of Jesus Christ as omnipresent in all, Jung saw it as an awaited incarnation within poor imperfect earthly humankind, which indeed was what Swedenborg himself understood by his New Church but saw it as already accomplished. Jung points out that Jesus himself in sending to his disciples "the spirit of truth," the Holy Ghost, envisages a continuing realization of God in his children, which amounts to a continuance of the Incarnation. He reminds his disciples that he had told them that they were "gods." The believers or the chosen ones are children of God, all "fellow-heirs with Christ." Of this teaching the fourth Gospel is full:

> "The indwelling of the Holy Ghost" means nothing less than an approximation of the believer to the status of God's son. One can therefore understand what is meant by the remark "you are gods." The deifying effect of the Holy Ghost is naturally assisted by the imago Dei stamped on the elect. God, in the shape of the Holy Ghost, puts up his tent in man, for he is obviously

minded to realize himself continually not only in Adam's descendants, but in an indefinitely large number of believers, and possibly in mankind as a whole.[21]

Only in suffering the limitations of the "empirical human being," Jung insists, can God truly suffer the human condition; for, in a Christ exempt from sin, he could not do so. Jung points out that, throughout the history of the church—both Catholic and Protestant—whereas the worship of the Son has been practiced and encouraged, the presence of the Holy Spirit within the soul has been played down, to say the least. Jung cites the instance of the banning of the writings of Meister Eckhart on account of certain passages in which this teaching is made too clear for the liking of the apostolic hierarchy. Again, Corbin supports Jung, commenting:

> the action of the Paraclete, metaphysically so important, is wholly undesirable for the good organization of the Church, for it eludes all control. In consequence there was to be energetic affirmation of the uniqueness of the event of the Incarnation, and the progressive indwelling of the Holy Spirit in man either discouraged or ignored. Whoever felt himself to be inspired by the Holy Spirit to "deviations" was a heretic, his extirpation and extermination both necessary and in accordance with Satan's liking.[22]

This is the Protestant point of view, shared by Jung, son of a Lutheran pastor; by Henry Corbin; by Swedenborg; and by William Blake. It is at the heart of the great and unresolved division within Christendom.

The millennial prophesies of Joachim of Flora have echoed throughout subsequent history his foretelling of a third phase of Christendom that he called the Age of the Holy Spirit, which was to follow the ages of the Father and of the Son. Within this tradition, Swedenborg and Blake are situated, and indeed so is Jung himself. Jung writes on the sending of the Paraclete:

> Since he is the Third Person of the Deity, this is as much as to say that God will be begotten in creaturely man. This implies a tremendous change in man's status, for he is now raised to sonship, and almost to the position of a man-god. With this the prefiguration in Ezekiel and Enoch, where, as we saw, the title "Son of Man" was already conferred on the creaturely man, is fulfilled. But that puts man, despite his continuing sinfulness, in the position of the mediator, the unifier of God and creature. Christ probably had this incalculable possibility in mind when he said, ". . . he who believes in me, will also do the works I do," and referring to the sixth verse of the Eighty-second Psalm, "I say, 'You are gods, sons of the Most High, all of you,'" he added, "and scripture cannot be broken."[23]

I have quoted Jung at length because his understanding of Christianity as a progressive revelation stands within the mystical mainstream represented by Joachim of Flora, Eckhart, Swedenborg, and Blake, even though Jung seems to have known little of the latter two, who certainly had no direct influence on Jung's own conclusions.

In some respects Swedenborg's Christianity lies within the mainstream of orthodoxy; he believed, for example, that Jesus Christ alone among humankind was resurrected in the natural body. Blake indeed reproached Swedenborg because he had not, in fact, taught anything new. In *The Marriage of Heaven and Hell,* Blake writes: "Now hear a plain fact: Swedenborg has not written one new truth. Now hear another: he has written all the old falsehoods" (MHH; K 157). What Blake chiefly held against Swedenborg was that he laid excessive stress on moral virtue, placing the virtuous in the heavens and the evildoers in the hells. Blake himself saw Divine Humanity as embracing the wholeness of life, both heaven and hell, reason and energy, the darkness and the light in a holiness and a wholeness beyond what humankind calls good and evil in terms of the moral laws of this world. Like Jung, Blake understood that there can be no completeness if any part of the totality of the Divine Human is excluded. It is probable that Blake did not, either, share Swedenborg's view of the unique and exceptional nature of the historical Jesus Christ. He does profess "the religion of Jesus," but by this he may not have meant Apostolic Christianity but the religion that Jesus himself practiced. Blake's view is that "Jesus, the Imagination," the Divine Human, is born, lives, and dies in every life, and the Resurrection is not of, but from, the carnal body. God is born in every birth, not one only; when Jehovah

> . . . stood in the Gates of the Victim, & he appeared
> A weeping Infant in the Gates of Birth in the midst of
> Heaven.

—he is born not in one but in all:

. . . a little weeping Infant pale reflected

Multitudinous in the Looking Glass of Enitharmon . . .

(J 63; K 697)

—that is, in the "mirror" of the natural world. The one Babe of the eternal Incarnation is reflected not in one, but in multitudes of births, in every birth. For Blake's Divine Humanity says,

. . . in Me all Eternity

Must pass thro' condemnation and awake beyond the grave.

(K 662)

Man is not once but continually redeemed in "the Body of Jesus"—that is, in the Divine Humanity in whom all participate; and the "Divine Similitude"—the face of God—is seen

In loves and tears of brothers, sisters, sons, fathers and friends

Which if Man ceases to behold, he ceases to exist.

(K 664)

The "Divine Family" is "as one Man"

. . . and they were One in Him. A Human Vision!

Human Divine, Jesus the Saviour, Blessed for ever and ever.

(K 667)

Thus, the "Divine Humanity" is not a single individual but a family; and Blake goes so far as to condemn explicitly the teaching that the Lord, or any of the "eternal states" that constitute the human universe is or ever could be represented by any single individual. In this Blake certainly goes beyond Swedenborg, at least in relation to the Jesus Christ of history. How strongly Blake held this view is clear from these lines from *Jerusalem*:

> Los cries: "No Individual ought to appropriate to
> Himself
> "Or to his Emanation [his feminine counterpart] any
> of the Universal Characteristics
> "Of David or of Eve, of the Woman or of the Lord,
> "Of Reuben or of Benjamin, of Joseph or Judah or
> Levi.
> "Those who dare appropriate to themselves Universal
> Attributes
> "Are the Blasphemous Selfhoods, & must be broken
> asunder.
> "A Vegetated Christ & a Virgin Eve are the Hermaph-
> roditic
> "Blasphemy, by his Maternal Birth he is that Evil-One
> "And his Maternal Humanity must be put off Eternally,
> "Lest the Sexual Generation swallow up Regen-
> eration."
>
> (J 90; K 736)

—and the passage ends with the invocation,

> "Come, Lord Jesus, take on thee the Satanic Body of
> Holiness."

The Divine Humanity is invoked to put on a generated body in order to transcend his natural humanity, transmitted by the mother. To Blake, mortal generation is a bind-

ing of an immortal spirit into the cruel bondage of
mortality:

> Thou, Mother of my Mortal part,
> With cruelty didst mould my Heart,
> And with false self-deceiving tears
> Didst bind my Nostrils, Eyes, & Ears:
> Didst close my Tongue in senseless clay,
> And me to Mortal Life betray.
> The Death of Jesus set me free.
> Then what have I to do with thee?
>
> (K 220)

This poem from *Songs of Experience* is far indeed from
those Christmas lullabies of the nativity to which we are
accustomed but is a concise summary of Swedenborg's
teaching. Readers unfamiliar with Swedenborg's view of
the place of the mother in the mystery of the Incarnation
must find Blake's treatment of the Incarnation in this and
other passages extremely puzzling. But the Leading Doctrines of the Church of the New Jerusalem, far from sup-
porting the view of the Immaculate Conception of the
Virgin Mary, see the mother as the means through which
Jesus Christ took on sin. Both Swedenborg and Blake had
confronted the question that was later to present itself to
Jung, of how the not-quite-human son of a mother herself
born without sin could experience the human condition.
If, as Swedenborg taught, Jesus came to "glorify his
human" by overcoming the successive temptations "admitted into his human from the mother" in order to "put
on a human from the Divine within him, which is the Divine Human, and the Son of God" (*Four Doctrines* 4, 64),

then the mother is indeed, as in Blake's poem, "cruel" and the source of evil, not of good. Swedenborg is quite categorical in his insistence that the natural humanity inherited by Jesus Christ from his earthly mother "cannot be transmuted into the Divine Essence nor can it be commixed with it . . . thus it follows that the Lord put off the human from the mother which, in itself, was like the human of another man, and thus material, and put on the human from the Father, which, in itself, was like His Divine, and thus substantial; and from which the Human was also made divine" (*Four Doctrines* 77)—not, be it understood, by the elevation of what Blake calls "a Vegetated Christ" but, on the contrary, by putting off his natural humanity. Blake summarizes the Swedenborgian teaching when he writes, of Jesus,

> He took on Sin in the Virgin's Womb,
> And put it off on the Cross & Tomb.
>                                    (EG; K 749)

Thus, in his doctrine that "the Lord put off the human from the Mother, and put on the Human from the Divine in himself which is called the father," Swedenborg anticipated and resolved Jung's later question as to the incompleteness of the Incarnation. What Jung saw as a future possibility Swedenborg and Blake saw as already accomplished in the mystery of the Incarnation, which had not hitherto been properly understood. The two lines just quoted are taken from a late poem by Blake entitled *The Everlasting Gospel*, a series of fragments that are, in fact, all expositions of Swedenborg's Leading Doctrines, a fact

which entirely confutes the often-propounded view of
Blake scholars that Swedenborg's influence is to be found
only in Blake's early works. This is by no means the case;
the influence of Swedenborg, if anything, is clearer in the
last works than in the first. One fragment expands at
length the necessity that the mother of Jesus should be a
vehicle of sins and not "a Virgin pure / With narrow Soul
& looks demure." Blake comes very close indeed to Jung
when he writes

> Or what was it, which he took on
> That he might bring salvation?
> A body subject to be tempted
> From neither pain or grief Exempted?
> Or such a body as might not feel
> The passions that with sinners deal?
>
> (EG)

Yet in affirming the indwelling of the Divine Human in
mankind, and the total humanity of Jesus in taking on a
fully human, fully sinful inheritance, how far are Swedenborg, and Blake, and Jung also for that matter, from any
humanistic intent of exalting the natural humanity—the
mortal selfhood—to a godlike status, usurping the name
of humanity from the divine principle in man and affirming the supremacy of the natural man. Swedenborg insists
that it is only through putting off his natural humanity
through temptations overcome, and finally on the cross,
that Jesus glorified the Divine Humanity of the Father.
Blake, who saw the divine image in every human face,
wrote:

The Spirit of Jesus is continual forgiveness of Sin: he who waits to be righteous before he enters into the Saviour's kingdom, the Divine Body, will never enter there. I am perhaps the most sinful of men. I pretend not to holiness: Yet I pretend to love, to see, to converse with daily as man with man, & the more to have an interest in the Friend of Sinners.

(K 621)

And finally Jung, who has most powerfully carried into our own day the mystery of the divine presence in every man, concludes his *Answer to Job* with these words, on the paradox of the divine presence that indwells "the ordinary mortal who is not free from original sin": "Even the enlightened person remains what he is, and is never more than his limited ego before the One who dwells within him, whose form has no knowable boundaries, who encompasses him on all sides, fathomless as the abysms of the earth and vast as the sky."

## Notes

1. Quotations from Blake's works are taken from *The Complete Works of William Blake*, edited by Geoffrey Keynes (London: Nonesuch Press, 1957; Oxford, UK: Oxford University Press, 1966). References in the text are cited by abbreviations for Blake's works, listed below; these sometimes include line or page numbers, followed by "K" and Keynes page number:

| | |
|---|---|
| AI | "Auguries of Innocence," from the Pickering Manuscript (c. 1803) |
| DC | *A Descriptive Catalogue* (1809) |
| EG | *The Everlasting Gospel* (c. 1818) |
| FZ | *Vala,* or *The Four Zoas* (1795–1804) |
| J | *Jerusalem* (1804–1820) |
| LAOC | *Laocoön* plate (c. 1820) |
| M | *Milton, a Poem in 2 Books* (1804–1808) |

MHH     *The Marriage of Heaven and Hell* (c. 1790–1793)
VLJ     *A Vision of the Last Judgment* (1810)
2. Genesis 1:26.

3. Annotations to [George] Berkeley's *Siris*: K 774

4. Henry Corbin (1903–1978) is considered one of the great Islamic scholars of the twentieth century. He was chair of Islamic Studies at the Sorbonne from 1954 to 1974 and also director of the department of Iranic Studies at the Institut franco-iranien in Tehcran. This essay was first presented as a lecture in 1985 at an annual conference established by Corbin.

5. See Henry Corbin, review of C. G. Jung's *Answer to Job*, in *La Revue de Culture Européen* 5 (1953).

6. Carl G. Jung, *Answer to Job*, trans. R. F. C. Hull, Bollingen Series XX, in *The Collected Works of C. G. Jung*, vol. 11 (Princeton, NJ: Princeton University Press, 1969), p. 669.

7. Ibid., p. 669n.

8. Ibid., p. 402, para. 631.

9. Job 19:25–26.

10. Jung, *Answer to Job*, p. 409, para. 648.

11. Blake's letter to Thomas Butts, 2 October 1800 (K 804–805).

12. "On Berkeley" (K 775).

13. John 17:21.

14. Romans 8:22.

15. Carl G. Jung, *Psychology and Alchemy*, trans. R. F. C. Hull, Bolligen Series XX, *The Collected Works of C. G. Jung*, vol. 12 (Princeton, NJ: Princeton University Press, 1969), p. 7, para. 7.

16. Ibid., pp. 11–12, para. 12.

17. Ibid., p. 14, para. 15.

18. Corbin, review in *Culture Européen*, p. 14. See also Jung, *Psychology and Alchemy*, p. 21, para. 24.

19. Matthew 25: 35–37.

20. Matthew 25: 37–40.

21. Jung, *Answer to Job*, para. 656.

22. Corbin, review in *Culture Européen*, p. 29.

23. Jung, *Answer to Job*, para. 692.

# DE
# COELO & INFERNO.

1. **U**BI Dominus de Confummatione Sæculi, quæ eſt ultimum tempus Ecclefiæ *(a)*, coram Diſcipulis loquitur, ad finem Prædictionum de fucceſſivis Statibus ejus quoad amorem & fidem *(b)*, ita dicit, " *Statim poſt afflictionem dierum iſtorum Sol obſcurabitur, & Luna non dabit lumen ſuum, & Stellæ cadent de Cælo, & potentiæ cælorum commovebuntur. Et tunc apparebit ſignum Filii hominis in Cælo; & tunc plangent omnes Tribus terræ: & videbunt Filium hominis venientem in nubibus Cæli cum potentia & gloria multa. Et emittet Angelos ſuos cum tuba & voce magna, & congrega᷄ bunt electos Ipſius a quatuor ventis, ab extremo cælorum uſque ad extremum illo᷄ rum,*" Matth: xxiv: 29. 30. 31. Qui fecundum fenſum literæ illa verba intelligunt, non aliter credunt, quam quod omnia illa fecundum deſcriptio᷄ nem in illo fenſu poſtremo tempore, quod vocatur Ultimum Judicium, eventura ſint; ita non ſolum quod Sol & Luna obſcurabuntur, & quod Stellæ cadent de Cœlo, quodque appariturum ſignum Domini in cœlo, & quod viſuri Ipſum in nubibus, & ſimul angelos cum tubis, ſed etiam fecundum prædictiones alibi, quod totus Mundus aſpectabilis periturus ſit, ac poſtea Novum Cœlum cum Nova Terra exſtiturum: in hac opinione ſunt plerique hodie intra Eccleſiam: ſed qui ita credunt, non ſciunt arcana quæ latent in ſingulis Verbi; in ſingulis enim Verbi eſt Senſus internus; in quo non naturalia & mundana, qualia ſunt quæ in fenſu literæ, ſed ſpiritualia & cœleſtia,

A 2

---

*Ex* Arcanis Coelestibus.

*(a)* Confummatio fæculi quod ſit ultimum tempus Eccleſiæ, n: 4535. 10672.
*(b)* Explicantur quæ Dominus de Confummatione fæculi, deque Adventu Ipſius, ita de fucceſſiva vaſtatione Eccleſiæ & de Ultimo judicio prædixerat apud Matthæum Cap: xxiv & xxv, in initiis ad Capita v ad xxiv Genef: & ibi n: 3353 ad 3356. 3486 ad 3489. 3650 ad 3655. 3751 ad 3759. 3897 ad 3901. 4056 ad 4060. 4129 ad 4231. 4332 ad 4335. 4422 ad 4424. 4635 ad 4638. 4661 ad 4664. 4807 ad 4810. 4954 ad 4959. 5063 ad 5071.

Opening page of first edition of *Heaven and Hell* (1758)

# The Reality of
# the Visionary World

## BY COLIN WILSON

here is a paradox involved in the basic quality of
human existence. Our hands touch solid objects,
our eyes see shapes and colors, our everyday hori-
zons are narrow; yet there are times when the soul seems
to stand on hilltops and to glimpse immense vistas of
meaning. This feeling is not confined to saints or poets or
philosophers—we all have it at certain moments of happiness and relaxation. It seems somehow *realer* than the triv-
ialities of everyday existence. And this is the paradox. For
surely *reality* means this world of solid objects that sur-
round us and the things they tell us about on television
news. The poet replies, "No, these things are not 'realer'
than the mystical vision; they are only *more close-up*." And
he continues to try to find his way back to the hilltops.
Many of the finest poets and artists of the nineteenth century died of exhaustion and despair at being unable to
find those higher levels again.

Until the seventeenth century, European civilization
was essentially Christian—which meant that people had a

clear idea of the meaning of human existence. There was a heaven above and a hell beneath, and we were suspended somewhere between the two, able to glimpse heaven or sink into hell. That meant, essentially, that there was a greater "Meaning" behind the trivial meanings of our everyday existence, and we felt that everything we did had an invisible significance, which would become clear when we reached the After Life.

Since then, it has sometimes seemed that science not only destroyed the religious myths but also their deeper meanings. If we believe in nothing but the material world, we become victims of the narrowness of our own consciousness. We are trapped in triviality. Religion gave us a reason for trying to reach the stars—for creating the magnificent spires and arches of Gothic cathedrals, the great masses of the renaissance composers, the stained glass of Chartres, the masterpieces of Michelangelo. Where there is a distance between heaven and earth, there is also a great vault in which the spirit can soar. When heaven descends to earth, poetry has to crawl on its hands and knees.

Swedenborg belonged to an age of faith, when the majority of people believed in angels and devils; less than a century later, German critics insisted that the Bible was merely a piece of imaginative fiction and that Jesus never existed. Intellectuals began to look back on the "age of faith" with nostalgia. Many of them—like Thomas Carlyle, Alfred Lord Tennyson, Ralph Waldo Emerson, Herman Melville—were men of religious feelings who were unable to accept traditional Christianity; they felt stranded in an emotional wasteland. In 1850, Emerson produced a long essay on Swedenborg in his *Representative Men,* treating him as one of the great mystical giants: "One of the . . . mastodons of literature he is not to be measured by whole colleges of ordinary scholars . . . Our books are false by being fragmentary . . . But Swedenborg is systematic and respective of the world in every sentence . . . his faculties work with astronomic punctuality, and this admirable writing is pure from all pertness or egoism." But he goes on to warn that to understand Swedenborg "requires almost a genius equal to his own."

At the age of fourteen, I was an ardent admirer of Emerson; I had expected his essays to be stuffy and was amazed to discover that they were clear, shrewd, and imbued with a kind of heroic individualism. *Representative Men* impressed me even more; so when I saw an old edition of Swedenborg's *True Christian Religion* in a Leicester bookshop, I saved up two weeks' pocket money and bought it. My disappointment was immense. It seemed to consist almost entirely of quotations from the scriptures and long discussions of their precise meaning. That seemed to me a sheer waste of time. The Bible might be an extraordinary historical and religious document; but I was convinced that it was "inspired" only in the same sense as Shakespeare's plays or Dante's *Divine Comedy.* So it seemed pointless to discuss its words as if they were mathematical propositions from which you could prove something.

And then there were those incredible sections called "Memorabilia," in which Swedenborg described his discussions with angels. Most of them read like parables; but apparently Swedenborg insisted that they had actually taken place. At which point, I decided that Swedenborg was a man whose brain had addled through too much brooding on religion—like the religious nuts who came to our front door with tracts and gramophones. I pushed the book into a corner of the bookcase and forgot about it.

Two years later, I discovered the poetry of William Blake and began to read everything I could find about him. It seemed that, in spite of some hostile remarks about Swedenborg, Blake had been strongly influenced by him. That was interesting, for Blake seemed to possess a healthy and skeptical intellect—not unlike that of Bernard Shaw. I borrowed Cyriel Sigstedt's *The Swedenborg Epic* from the library and was startled to discover that Swedenborg began life as a scientist and engineer and that everyone who met him agreed that he was a polite, logical man with a kindly manner and a sense of humor.

And then there were those baffling stories of his second sight. About to sit down to dinner in Gothenburg, Swedenborg turned pale and told the company that a great fire had just broken out in Stockholm, three hundred miles away. Two hours later, he said: "Thank heavens, the fire is now under control. It had almost reached my doorstep." Two days later, a letter arrived from Stockholm confirming everything he had said. That, of course, is "second sight," and many people possess it. The same might be said for the story of how he helped Madame Marteville, the widow of the Dutch ambassador, who had received a bill from a silversmith, although she was convinced that her husband had paid it; a few days later, Swedenborg told her that the receipted bill could be found in a secret drawer of a certain bureau. The bill was found where he had described it. Swedenborg claimed he had obtained the information direct from the deceased ambassador in the spirit world. He made the same claim about a message from the deceased brother of the Queen of Sweden; when Swedenborg described to her the contents of the last letter she had sent to her brother, the queen exclaimed "No one but God knows this secret."

Medieval culture was based on saints and visionaries; modern culture is based on Freud, Darwin, and Marx. We envy Dante and Fra Angelico for having a heaven to soar into. And we recognize that people like Blaise Pascal, Blake, and Swedenborg were attempting to reassert the basic reality of heaven and so to create the conditions in which the spirit could soar. Our materialistic philosophy has made us slaves of the trivial. Yet how could Swedenborg and Blake begin to undermine this materialism? Only by asserting the solid *reality* of the visionary world. Blake said he saw a tree full of angels. Possibly he was lying—or exaggerating. But what of a man who says, "No, it is just a tree." Is he not lying too? Perhaps Blake's angels are closer to the truth . . .

The argument is fair, but it begs the question of Swedenborg's visions. He insisted that he was *not* exaggerating or telling lies or speaking in parables. Yet, in another book, he describes the inhabitants of the moon, Mars and Venus (admittedly, their spiritual inhabitants, not solid creatures). This brings us back to the problem that baffled his contemporaries. Was he a genuine visionary, a God-inspired prophet? Or was he suffering from delusions? Of one thing there can be no doubt: Swedenborg's contemporaries were in no position to answer that question. At that time, there were only two possible schools of thought: scientists who would dismiss the whole thing as superstition and orthodox Christians who would admit that, in theory at any rate, there was no reason why a "chosen vessel" should not be taken on a circular tour of heaven.

In the late nineteenth century, science would begin to admit a third possibility: that the mind contains unexplored depths in which the visions might have originated. Freud's interpretation of that possibility would have been wholly negative: that the visions were basically some form of mental illness or compensation mechanism. But his ex-disciple Carl Jung suggested altogether more interesting possibilities. The subconscious mind is not a cellar filled with decaying rubbish and repressed passions. In fact, we make a mistake in thinking of the subconscious as something "inside" us. Perhaps the truth may be that we are inside *it*, like fishes in the sea. This "sea" contains many universal symbols, or archetypes, which are common to us all. What Jung was asserting was that there are things in the mind that have an *independent existence*, just like the objects around us in the material world.

Jung developed a technique called "active imagination" that enabled him to descend into his own mind and hold conversations with "imaginary" beings. There was a character whom he called Philemon, and Jung says, "In my fantasies I held conversations with him, and he said things which I had not consciously thought. *For I observed clearly that it was he who spoke, not I*" [my italics].

In 1953, Aldous Huxley experimented with the drug mescaline sulphate, which produced the effect of intensifying his perception of reality and making him aware that, when we think we are "seeing" the world, we are actually perceiving it through a thick mental blanket of our own concepts and desires. And in a book whose title—*Heaven and Hell*—seems to be a deliberate evocation of Swedenborg, he stated, "Like the earth of a hundred years ago, our mind still has its darkest Africas, its unmapped Borneos and Amazonian basins." Huxley went on to say that these unexplored continents of the mind contain creatures as strange and improbable as the giraffe and duck-billed platypus.

These observations, while they leave certain basic questions unanswered, nevertheless enable us to understand that the words *vision* and *reality* are not mutually exclusive. Bernard Shaw was hinting at the same thing when he made his Joan of Arc say that God speaks to us through the imagination. He was using the word *imagination* in Blake's sense. ("Vision or Imagination is a Representation of what Eternally Exists . . .")

The same point is made very clearly in *Essay on the Origin of Thought* by Jurij Moskvitin, a Danish philosopher. Moskvitin observes that when he lay with his eyes half-closed in the sunlight, looking at the sky through his eyelashes, he became aware of a fascinating spectrum of colors and of geometric patterns. Gradually, he accustomed himself to "focusing" these patterns at will and concluded that they were made up of "dancing sparks." Further observation convinced him that the sparks were not really independent; they were prominent parts of certain "smoke-like forms." He explains this with a useful image: if you look at the sea in the sunlight, the breaking waves seem to be tipped with light; but that, if you stare hard, these "sparks" are seen to be part of rings and nets that move over the water. He goes on to say that the smokelike forms "became the elements of waking dreams, forming persons, landscapes, strange mathematical forms . . ." It struck Moskvitin that much religious art seems to contain perceptions of these forms. "The actual experience is like a Rorschach test—always interpreted according to what a man has in his mind . . . This is the derivation of all ghosts, elves and demons."

We are inclined to think of our perception as a kind of mirror, merely reflecting the reality around us. You are like a person looking through a reflecting telescope; light travels from that book to the mirror and is reflected down to "you," looking through the eyepiece. Moskvitin is saying that in perception, we "project" some kind of magic element from behind the eyes: the world is not reflected in a mirror but in something more like the moving surface of the sea, and we infer the reality through a skill developed over a lifetime.

In his book on Swedenborg, *The Presence of Other Worlds*, Wilson Van Dusen advances suggestions about Swedenborg's visions that are based on Van Dusen's own experience of meditation and "hypnagogic states" (i.e., states that exist on the borderline of sleeping and waking). Most of us observe such states briefly, then fall asleep. Van Dusen insists that it is possible to remain awake, observing "mental processes occur spontaneously." Like Jung, he notes that "there is enough self-awareness in the hypnagogic state to remember, record and even talk to inner processes." These views are close to the reality of Swedenborg's visionary experiences. Beyond the hypnagogic state lies the trance state, in which the "naked self," so to speak, learns to descend into the inner world without falling asleep. consciousness is intensified, but bodily awareness is lost.

Although we certainly know more about these inner states than Swedenborg's contemporaries, we still have only half the answer, perhaps even less. Jung believed that Philemon was, in fact, a "wiser self," representing superior insight. Other modern psychologists have made use of the concept of the "superconscious mind." For if the mind has its subconscious "cellar," may it not also have a super-conscious "attic," a part of the mind that possesses deeper insight and higher knowledge than the "everyday self"? Many water diviners believe that their dowsing rods respond to the knowledge of the superconscious mind; this seems to be confirmed by the fact that a good dowser can divine for anything, simply by "tuning in." If he is dowsing for oil or iron ore, his rod will ignore water. And so it seems probable, at least, that Swedenborg's angels were, like Philemon, representatives of his higher self and that his visions of heaven and hell were symbolic representations of real inner states encountered by the soul after death. (According to Swedenborg, the world after death consists entirely of inner states and has no external space and time like our world.)

At the same time, we must admit that it is possible that Swedenborg's angels were, in fact, higher beings, and not "symbols" created by the mind. Van Dusen states flatly that "these inner states raise the issue of the presence of other spiritual beings interacting in our lives." Novels like *The Exorcist* have certainly popularized the possibility that demonic forces might exist independent of the human mind. When we begin to examine recorded cases of "possession," we again become aware of the ambiguities that are concealed by our clear, scientific concepts. Jung began his career as a psychologist by observing a female cousin who seemed to possess two completely distinct personalities. Psychologists who have studied cases of dual—and even multiple—personalities conclude that there are strange ways in which the self can split into several mutually independent personalities. This seems to suggest that we are dealing simply with a Freudian problem of repression. But then, how do we explain how "possessed" people occasionally speak in languages of which they have no knowledge—for example, Latin?

An experience recorded by the "paranormal" researcher Alan Vaughan may help to throw light on one aspect of Swedenborg's powers. At the beginning of *Patterns of Prophecy*, Vaughan explains how he became interested in the power of foreseeing the future. Experimenting alone with a ouija board, Vaughan found himself "possessed" by a neurotic woman, whose "voice" somehow got inside his head. Experimenting with another friend, Vaughan suddenly experienced a second presence inside his head—this time a benevolent presence, which made him write out a message: "Each of us has a spirit while living. Do not meddle with the spirits of the dead." Suddenly, a third presence seemed to rise inside him with a flood of energy, driving out both the other two. In this moment of "dispossession," Vaughan experienced a tremendous elation and well-being and realized that he could read other people's minds and see into the future "through some kind of extended awareness." The experience led to his interest in prophetic dreams.

Quite obviously, we stand on the borderline of a new domain of knowledge, and we know as little of it as Marco

Polo knew of China or the earliest explorers of Africa. One thing seems clear: there are mental states in which we can glimpse vistas of knowledge that remain concealed from us in "everyday consciousness." Our great mistake lies in supposing that the kind of "knowledge" we acquire slowly over a lifetime is real, ultimate knowledge. We are probably like blind men, born into a world in which we have to find our way around by the sense of touch—and by the use of walking sticks, scientific extensions of sensory knowledge. Like the citizens of H. G. Wells's country of the blind, we take it as a law of nature that only certain forms of knowledge are possible (for example, that you cannot know when someone is approaching until he or she is close enough to hear). Vaughan's sudden glimpse of a power to read other people's minds and see into the future seems to be the equivalent of "sight" in our blind men.

Swedenborg always possessed unusual intellectual powers and a remarkable ability to concentrate for long periods. He went through great spiritual crises in his sixth decade, and it seems probable that his frantic struggles led to the activation of this "new faculty." Books like *Divine Providence* and *Divine Love and Wisdom* were not written in some confused state of religious mania but in a strange state of visionary clarity that led him to write at top speed to try to convey everything he saw. He lived in a religious age; his father was a bishop; he had studied the Bible since childhood. It was, therefore, natural that his visions expressed themselves in terms of the Bible. If he had been brought up on the works of Shakespeare or Dante, no doubt his ideas would have expressed themselves in the form of gigantic commentaries on Shakespeare's tragedies or the *Divine Comedy*. The chief obstacle to the modern understanding of Swedenborg is that few of us can take the Bible for granted in the way that our great-grandfathers did. This is a sad reflection on the modern age; and it means that, if anyone is anxious to reach some understanding of Swedenborg's strange mystical vision, that reader will have to take the trouble to become acquainted with this vital part of our literary heritage.

For the beginner, patience is certainly necessary. Originally written in Latin, by a man whose previous works had all been scientific treatises, Swedenborg's theological works make an initial impression of dullness. However, once you have grown accustomed to his habit of mind, they are readable enough; and a good modern translation makes a considerable difference. Swedenborg is no cranky religious messiah, demanding total credence and allegiance. He admits that he is an intellectual, who prefers to be understood rather than believed. One of the "Memorabilia" in his *True Christian Religion* describes his encounter (in the spirit world, of course), with a preacher whose religious obscurities are punctuated with the statement that it is important to "keep our reason in subjection to faith." This view makes Swedenborg see red. Swedenborg tells the priest that there is no point in talking about "mysteries" unless you are prepared to try and look inside them and try to understand them. The priest is furious, and the congregation make their way home contentedly, "intoxicated with paradoxes, bewildered with verbiage and enveloped in darkness."

This very quickly becomes plain as you read Swedenborg: he is obsessed with making himself clear. No one ever cared less about trying to impress with tricks of style or poetic images. Compared to some of the Catholic saints—Theresa of Avila, for example—he seems to be almost a rationalist.

*Heaven and Hell* has always been Swedenborg's most popular book because it can be read with a minimum of such preparation. Yet even this book has its pitfalls. Emerson said of it: "A vampire sits in the seat of the prophet, and turns with gloomy appetite to the images of pain. Indeed, a bird does not more readily weave its nest . . . than this seer of the souls substructs a new hell and pit, each more abominable than the last . . . Except Rabelais and Dean Swift, nobody ever had such science of filth and corruption." This makes Swedenborg sound like an old-fashioned hellfire preacher. Yet the Swedish genius August Strindberg, passing through a severe psychological crisis that brought him to the brink of madness, found sanity in *Heaven and Hell,* recognizing that Swedenborg had described the succession of mental states and decisions that had brought him to the brink of his own private hell. Strindberg became increasingly convinced that Swedenborg was a visionary genius who had foreseen the spiritual torments of the twentieth century.

When the psychologist William James passed through a crisis of depression and panic anxiety, he used Swedenborg's term "vastation" to describe the state. And this was natural enough since his own father, Henry James, Sr., had been brought back from the brink of mental and physical breakdown by the discovery of Swedenborg's works. The breakdown had come upon the elder James suddenly and without warning one day after eating a comfortable dinner, sitting idly at the table and feeling rather pleased with himself. "Suddenly—in a lightning flash, as it were—fear came upon me, and trembling, which made all my bones to shake. To all appearances it was a perfectly insane and abject terror, without ostensible cause, and only to be accounted for, to my perplexed imagination, by some damned shape squatting invisible to me within the precincts of the room, and raying out from his fetid personality influences fatal to life. . . ."

The depression and terror of James, Sr., continued for two years, until a woman friend told him that he was suffering from what Swedenborg called "vastation" and that it could well be the gateway to some inward transformation. James, Sr., was so ill that he was not allowed to read; nevertheless, he bought two volumes of Swedenborg and kept them by his bed, dipping into them for a few sentences at a time. Finally, he began to read avidly. "I read from the first with palpitating interest. My heart divined, even before my intelligence was prepared to do justice to the books, the unequalled amount of truth to be found in them. Imagine a fever patient, sufficiently restored of his malady to think of something besides himself, suddenly transported where the free airs of heaven blow upon him, and the sound of running water refreshes his jaded sense; and you have a feeble image of my delight in reading. . . ." James, Sr., became convinced that the cause of all his suffering had been "the profound unconscious death I bore about in my . . . selfhood."

Swedenborg's crises had brought him close to insanity; this is undoubtedly why he possesses such extraordinary power to bring peace to tormented souls like Strindberg and James. "One thunderstorm followed another. My enduring these storms was a matter of brute strength. Others have been shattered by them—Nietzsche and

Holderlin, and many others. But there was a demoniac strength in me, and from the beginning there was no doubt in my mind that I must find the meaning of what I was experiencing . . ." This is not Swedenborg speaking— as the reference to Nietzsche and Holderlin must have made plain—but Carl Jung. Yet no one who has read both Jung and Swedenborg can doubt that it was the mystic, not the psychologist, who ventured furthest into the depths of this alien world that lies inside us. At a time when rationalism is dying on us, a teacher of the reality of the Will is revelant as never before.

WILSON VAN DUSEN

# A Mystic Looks
# at Swedenborg

## BY WILSON VAN DUSEN

*The doctrines simply are not much use to me unless I know what
it is in my own experience that they are talking about.*
—George Dole, from *Messenger* review of *Arcana Coelestia*

*There is the closest relation between the mode of apprehension
and the thing apprehended.*
—Gabriel Marcel, from *Creative Fidelity*

### The Nature of Mysticism

I use the word *mystic* in its simplest and most basic
sense. A mystic is one who experiences God. There
are other associated meanings and very complex
analyses in religious encyclopedias, but they all rest in
this—the experience of God. Some might ask, "Don't all
people experience God?" And I would answer yes, but
many are not aware of it. The mystic is aware of it.

Perhaps I need to underline the verb *experience*. It is
quite a bit more than simply thinking about God or

addressing God. God becomes manifest, obvious. And by using the present tense, I also mean to imply that the experience tends to be ongoing. Having experienced God once, one acquires a taste for it. The mystic learns how to find his or her way back into that communion.

In this essay I'll cite my own experience merely because it is handy for me, with some reference to the experience of others. My aim is to make the spiritual experience familiar enough to be recognizable to the reader. After establishing this base, we will then see how this is reflected in Swedenborg. The parallel is not simply in the fact that Swedenborg talks about God. Most theological writing concerns God, but most also seems quite flat and unmystical to me. On the other hand, certain music, literature, paintings, and other art forms easily bring me back to the experience of the Divine. The relevance of mystical experience to Swedenborg's own has more to do with a mode of experiencing than with mere content matter.

If someone asked when I first became aware that I was a mystic, I would date it to early adolescence. We lived on the top floor of several flats, and I soon discovered I could climb a ladder to the roof. In the crowded world of San Francisco, I found that the rooftop offered me an expansive private world. The dusk of evening was always the nicest time. Lights were dimming and my thoughts soared. I came back repeatedly to the feeling of the oneness of things. All the city lights, all the dusky shapes, all the sounds were One Life. I knew also I was this One Life looking at and admiring the One Life. The basic feeling was awe or reverence. No matter what the difficulties of the day, in the evening, under the stars, it was indeed wonder-full.

On the front of the roof was a curved decoration. It was high enough so that I could lean on it and safely look down on the street. I remember lovingly touching the tar paper with awe. The very reality of substance seemed miraculous. I heard the sound of a distant dog bark. I was in such a sense of oneness that it was as though I heard my own life. I remember hearing a screen door squeak and slam shut somewhere; and with that simple sound, I knew the design of creation. I remember swearing to myself that no matter what happens in life, I would always come back to the peace of evening. And, in a real sense, by writing of it, I am back to that peace. I was so awestruck by the wonder of existence. There was also no sense of ego—no me-versus-it. Me and it were one.

*Reverence* is the term that would come to me now to describe the experience, but it would not have then. I had yet to learn that religion and God really existed. My father was an atheist, and my mother disdained all religion, even though she was raised a Catholic. She had had a hard life. She had said many times, "If there was a God, he would be unspeakably horrible." I had heard church services on the radio, but they didn't impress me. The preachers sounded like pompous salesmen, selling the Word instead of cars.

At that time my experience was nameless. I can remember the book that first suggested to me I was not alone, that there were others out there with similar experiences. My first five-cent book purchase was Thomas Troward's

*Edinburgh Lectures in Mental Science.*[1] I was struck by the
wonder of money, if it could buy treasures like that.
Thomas Troward was a member of the New Thought
Movement. For the first time, I saw echoes of my experience in print: "But because the universal personalness is
the root of all individual personalities, it finds its highest
expression in response to those who realize its personal
nature."[2] Yes, that's it. A spiritual moment is immensely
personal. I didn't hear any of the religious radio pro-
grams say that. "He must realize that the whole process is
that of bringing the universal within the grasp of the individual by raising the individual to the level of the universal, and not vice-versa."[3] Yes, yes! So when I see the design
of all in the sound of a screen door, it is the universal.
Everything I saw, heard, or touched spoke of the universal. It was a great comfort to discover, at last, that I was not
alone. Others have realized the same thing.

But, in a way, the experience was frustrating. It was like
standing on the edge of a vast sea of mystery, feeling that
it was all here, yet I wanted something specific. I'd ask the
universal for guidance in my life and then chide it for its
lack of specificity. All wasn't enough; I wanted something
more!

But the idea of the oneness of all things took firm root.
It found countless echoes later, in the ecologist's concern
for life, in the universality of humanity, for examples.
When I was young one of my favorite fantasies was that I
was making speeches to the world on peace and the fel-
lowship of humanity. I had a whole binder of what
seemed, at the time, like very inspired lectures. In later
years, I burned them as a bit too adolescent to keep. But it

still happens that the theme of the universality of life can easily bring tears to my eyes. It is something I feel so strongly that my reason has to stand aside. I know I'm I and you're you and that much separates and distinguishes us. But that's the job of reason, to cut things up and set them apart. It doesn't matter. I've experienced the one-ness of All. It became apparent to me that life could either be taken apart or experienced as a one. The experience of oneness was the more fundamental, satisfying, and powerful. It was the truth. All this taking apart is secondary, flat, and trivial in comparison.

You might wonder what the mystical experience does to personal identity. Sensing the All, would I not be greater than most who don't do this? Not in the least. Sensing the All, I am the equal of all—the equal of tar paper, a dog's bark, and stars. I would say the experience relaxes the personal identity down to the point where it doesn't matter. Later I was impressed by the Greek expression *En to Pan*, "the One is the All."

Over the years, it gradually dawned on me that my experience was religious and that the Universal One was another name for God. You see, I had these kinds of experiences before names, even before speech or words. Though I began this essay with an account from adolescence, I can recall an experience all the way back in infancy, when I was still in a crib, possibly around the age of one. I lay there with my head turned to the side. Sunlight was streaming though the window. Motes of dust floated and turned in the beam of sunlight. Fixing on them, I saw endless rainbows of color. The feeling was of ecstasy and awe. Later I learned in my study of psychoanalysis that this

identification with everything is common in children—
that it was a childish quality I'd apparently failed to out-
grow! Be that as it may, I found the roots of mystical
experience can exist before words, concepts, religious
training, before all the obscuring machinations of the
world. I suspect these experiential roots are pretty much
universal; they occur in all people. But in various ways our
education and acculturation can obscure them. The center can be forgotten.

In some way, my memory was turned around. My experience of the All became my foundation. Later, people
were surprised when I said I could far more easily doubt
my own existence than I could doubt God's. My own existence seems variable, hard to grasp, doubtful, and really
trivial. The All is everything. Perhaps by some bit of luck
(another term is *God's grace*), I retained the memory of
what others also knew and misplaced or forgot. In some
way, I feel obliged to describe the mystical experience so
that others may recover it. So here I will describe my adult
way of returning to it, which may also work for you. I've
been in and out of mystical experiences so often that it
has finally become clear how to find my way back. It can
be done anywhere, at any time. But there are certain ne-
cessities. I cannot be rushed nor in pain. The mood is one
of no hurry, endless time. I feel very open. I'll accept
whatever is given. It is the opposite of making demands
on God. The mood is one of openness and play. Just for
the fun, I feel like stopping here and admiring the flowers. Long ago I discovered it is the heart of aesthetic experience. How best to appreciate what is before you but by
stopping, looking, being open to what is suggested?

I had a group of alcoholic women contend that this could not be done within the bare walls of an institution. So I had them dwell intensely on the floor. One noticed a crack in the cement; and, in describing what it suggested to her, she came to a tearful description of her life pattern. Everything reveals if we are patient with it.

The whole of existence is like looking at a painting. I am regarding Van Gogh's second self-portrait. At first, I take in the obvious details: his face is angular and bearded; his clothes are rude, those of a peasant; the blue background swirls around his head with areas of chaos. There's a remarkable, quiet intensity in the face. Though closed-mouthed and mute, the intensity is almost wild, brooding. And this is the center of the man. He has painted his very nature. I empathize with the power of his struggle. In the mystical mood, I allow all there is to speak, to affect me. If I had to train mystics, I would certainly consider using art appreciation as a first step. For in it is the foundation of letting things reveal themselves to you.

But you may say this is merely aesthetic and not religious. The aesthetic is a step into the doorway of the religious. Its basic attitude is one of appreciation. It leads to awe and respect. It is the practice of openness to what is here. Like the aesthetic person, the mystic is in an appreciation of things as they are. This moment is perfect. It is all here, all there is.

There is a tremendous nowness to the mystical experience. It is as though all there ever was passes through this present into all there ever will be. One rests in such a moment. Questions have no place. Doubts are absent. Here, thus, it is. I once asked God for a sign of his existence. God answers in direct knowing, beyond words. His answer was, in effect, "Is not the whole of existence sign enough?" Well, yes, that's a pretty good one: existence—yes, I'd call that a substantial sign!

My existence is among these signs. So sometimes I just look at and admire my hand. Interesting form. Skin a little wrinkled because I'm aging. A real marvel how it is animated. Look at it writing here. Marvelous. I wonder what words are and how my hand works. I am mystery, looking at mystery, appreciating mystery. The very essence of mystical experience is to appreciate this fully—what is. Does it plague me that I am a mystery? No. I appreciate it. How far this is from egotism or Swedenborg's term *proprium*. No egotism, because I know beyond my understanding that the same life animates the pine tree in my backyard that animates me. What a delightfully pervasive mystery. What an honor to be an equal to pine trees, grass, and clouds.

I've described the mood and attitude that leads to mystical experience—taking the time to be open and thoroughly appreciate what is before you. But there are also deeper hallmarks of the mystical experience. Meaning is given, *noetic*. You suddenly realize something that is prior to thought, before any reasoning. You might just *know* that God is present. If someone asks how or where, you would have nothing to point to. This knowing can vary from a gentle suggestion to an absolute certainty. Outside that experience the subject himself can doubt it. "Was God really present?" But during the noetic givenness of knowing, doubt or questioning is not possible. I've even formulated my biggest questions and written them down, only to find my own sheet of questions rather ridiculous during the experience of God. One of the reasons I've written for many years and barely said anything of this experience is that it is sacred and beyond doubt.

I recall a woman who had a sudden, unexpected experience of God, lasting probably less than five seconds. She described it to a nun, who remarked, "You probably just had a digestive upset." The woman spent decades studying mysticism and trying to return to the experience; but, after the nun's rejection, she rarely told anyone of it. She now trains priests in the deeper aspects of religious experience. The mystical experience is so characterized by direct knowing that I'd call into question an experience where God talks aloud to a person.

The experience is up through the core of one's being. Words are not necessary. I once saw an angelic figure with wings crossed in front as though to conceal something. I wondered what was concealed. Suddenly, the answer came flooding in, but not in words. I was just given to know. The hidden secret was that there is no death. Nowhere in the whole of existence is there death. You are struck with not only the words but also the full ramifications of them. People think of death as real. The angel revealed the deeper truth; no one ever dies. And like waves and ripples the full ramifications play on the consciousness. In Raymond Moody's cases of people who "died" on the operating table and later were revived, many reported meeting a radiant figure who communicated by direct mind-to-mind knowing.[4] A parallel in ordinary experience is the way lovers sense so much before anything is said. In sharp contrast, when people who are hallucinating meet demons of hell, they talk endlessly but they say little! The more powerful the feeling that goes with direct knowing, the more I'd suspect it is just plain truth. Often in these experiences symbols are given, and, at the same time, the meanings of the symbols are given. A meaning can be so nonverbal that the person receiving it may have difficulty putting it into words. In these cases, I'd say it is therapeutic and useful to draw what was seen and attempt to extract and put into words all the information. Otherwise, the ordinary consciousness may later look at what was given and translate it into something much less significant than it was at the time (e.g., "I saw an angel and I guess it meant so and so"). But going back to the experience, one finds it packed with meaning. I was once given a simple hand gesture of two fingers extended and its meaning. I was thrilled years later to see it in an old painting in the Eastern Orthodox Church.

William James writes about the noetic:

> Although so similar to states of feeling, mystical states seem to those who experience them to also be states of knowledge. They are states of insight into depths of knowledge. They are states of insight into depths of truth unplumbed by the discursive intellect. They are illuminations, revelations, full of significance and importance, all inarticulate though they remain; and as a rule they carry with them a curious sense of authority for aftertime.[5]

William James also describes the mystical experience as "ineffable," or impossible to describe in words. I would not go so far as to say this. With care, one can describe the state. It's just that one can't fully convey the state in words because, as he says, it is more like states of feeling than of intellect.

## The Several Paths Are One Path

Having experienced a remarkable state, I was naturally curious to look at what the world's literature had to say of it. There are a number of scholarly compilations—collections and commentaries on what mystics have to say. Other than a few touching quotes from real mystics, these commentaries fall quite flat for me. Those writing them often draw conclusions that are just untrue, possibly because they haven't had the experience. They also tend to make a basically simple and direct experience quite complex, constructing stages, and stages within stages of the experience. Yet the real experience is terribly simple and straightforward.

In great contrast, the work of actual mystics often soars for me. Among these I'd list Plotinus, Khalil Gibran, Saint Theresa of Lisieux, Jakob Böhme, the Zen Buddhists, some Hindu works, and Omar Khayyam. Notice that this listing ranges across several religions. Mystics are dealing with universal truth revealed in most, and perhaps all, religions. Even though the content of these authors seems different—Gibran is in verse; Saint Theresa describes her relationship to Christ; Plotinus the Greek, like Jakob Böhme, presents a soaring intellectual understanding—they have the power of one who has been there.

In my experience, mystics have no difficulty recognizing other mystics. Because their eye is on the universal, they see beyond historical and doctrinal differences. I've often been asked by individuals whether their experience of God was true. Let me cite an unusual case to illustrate the process. I was at a Christian church gathering at a camp in the mountains. A minister's wife indicated she wanted to speak to me. As a practiced clinical psychologist, I could see that great feeling was involved. She hesitated to speak. Finally, I got her to tell her story.

One day a friend came to see her, bearing the message that her deceased father loved her. Suddenly, the situation opened up for her. She knew beyond doubt that this man, in the body of a known friend, was actually God, and God came to repair the relationship with her father. She had been emotionally alienated from her father. She asked me if this was a true experience of God, even though inwardly she knew beyond doubt it was. I felt a tremendous impact in her story. We both struggled unsuccessfully with tears. My response was that her story had the ring of truth to it, though I had never before seen the form of her experience—God coming in the body of a friend. God is able to come in any form, even the form of a friend. The incident essentially did good: it brought her into loving relationship with her father.

The woman's story had all of the hallmarks I look for in a genuine experience of God. The people hesitate to speak. What they have to say is powerfully sacred to them. It is the opposite of bragging: they would rather say nothing happened than to have the sacred rejected. The experience is linked to powerful feeling, which indicates to me that it comes from beyond mere intellect, from beyond the manipulations of consciousness. It is as though the very source of life is touched and shaken. Finally, I ask whether the experience does good. If so, I believe it is from God. I affirmed, as she already inwardly felt, that the experience was quite genuine.

What you often find, as was true of her, is that the mystical experience can be so powerful and otherworldly that the subject is somewhat at a loss as to what to do with it. I saw she was having difficulty integrating the experience. She said she went to the bishop of her church afterward, and he so discredited the experience that she swore to herself never to speak again of religious feeling in church! I took the opposite tack. Given that God was trying to repair the bond between her and her father, I asked that she prayerfully dwell on the love between them. I reinforce the trend in the experience. I try to act in concert with the tendencies shown by God. Countless bishops and psychotherapists could not kill the inner life of her experience. But in a few moments, I could strike a sentient chord merely by recognizing and reinforcing the quality of the experience given her.

I relate this incident to illustrate several things. I believe mystics can easily see and empathize with genuine experience in others, regardless of religious differences, no matter how unusual the form. I also think it something of a crime for someone to invalidate the depth of experience in others. It would have been far better if the bishop had said, "I don't know if your experience was really of God," for actually he didn't know.

Would I call this woman a mystic? Potentially, yes. She had had only one experience, but treating this one in a positive way would encourage her to open to others. She was just at the entrance of the house; she had yet to move in and become comfortable in the house. This woman's story also illustrates that the mystical experience is not totally ineffable, beyond description. Difficult to convey, yes; impossible, no. Moreover, in attempting to do so, others who hear of it might rethink their own sacred experiences and renew their belief in the wonders that have been given to them.

Follow, if you will, a fantasy of mine. Suppose I am able to encourage many people to describe their sacred experiences. I compile and publish a newsletter of these, and we convene to discuss them. In these meetings, the mood is one of acceptance of and respect for even the tiniest traces of sacredness in each other's experience. Because one describes, others recognize similar experiences in themselves. Because we accept and express and share these, new experiences arise and are shared. Mystical experience becomes common, and we are able to explore the length and breadth of it. A fantasy? Not entirely.

I've seen Teen Challenge sessions in which a similar situation occurred. All of the members present had been drug addicts picked up while down and out on the street. Because the group had expectations that the experience of Christ would occur, it did frequently. I recall one addict saying he watched in amazement as his hands poured heroin down the toilet. In that moment, he knew that Christ controlled him.

I have also seen Teen Challenge members speak to religious groups and frighten them. Most people's experience of religion is cool, rational, controlled. These people really believe, and they frighten people of a cool religion. For a similar reason, in the history of mysticism, it was fairly common for mystics to write anonymously (as did Swedenborg at first) or to come into conflict with the church (Teilhard de Chardin), or to write their experiences in a partly disguised form (*The Rubaiyat* of Omar Khayyam).

So, let me alter my fantasy above. Only mystics (of any religion) may enter our circle, and we share with each other only. But the underlying theme of my fantasy is that we share and respect experiences of God and thereby encourage others to recognize it in their life. In this day and age, I find that what is missing from and repressed in many people's lives is the sacred, not sexuality, as some maintain.

Why? At first, one might suggest we tend to hold back a sacred experience because we don't want others to scoff at it. The bishop's put-down of the woman discussed previously is a good example. The experience is particularly delicate if one has had only one or a few experiences. This is a partial reason for repressing the sacred. But there is another reason that has to do with the inward nature of the experience. What opens up in the person is the deepest root of life itself. It is one's life. Would we hand a scalpel to a passing stranger to perform surgery on us? The experience is our life, our very life. It often repels even the skeptical probing of the subjects themselves. That is, the experience can seem alien and incredible to even the person who has it. There is a great difference between the person who is moved in one sacred moment and the same person in the workaday world. In the light of day, that transcendent experience can be questioned and doubted by the subject who had it. Did it really happen? Was that God or digestive upset? It is uncomfortable to doubt it. It is like pinching oneself unnecessarily. So an uneasy peace settles.

I believe that, in the most inward sense, there is a natural protection around the sacred. At the very worst, the experience will totally disappear from memory rather than leave the sacred to be permanently questioned. So the barriers to assault on it are both internal and external. I don't want it to be laughed at, so I won't tell others. It is somehow wrong even for me to question it, so I'll not do so. It takes respect for the sacred by one person to open it up to expression in another. The woman who reacted to the bishop's put-down wasn't simply a petulant woman. The sacred protects itself, so she resolved never to expose real religious feeling in church again. I don't fully understand how the sacred protects itself. But I suspect that, if we could see its full ramifications, we'd be surprised at its artful, in-depth protection. I am so convinced that the sacred is the very root and source of life itself that I'm sure some have died rather than expose it (e.g., the early Christian martyrs). The doubts of others are rather easy to fend off: simply keep quiet about it. Internal doubt is another matter.

I would not be at all surprised to learn that one day madness itself comes from turning against the early budding of mystical experience in a person. Why do I say this? Because, in madness, I often see a strange tangle of essentially religious elements turned back on itself. It would be better not to have the experience of God than to harm it in any way. At the very least, the person who has it would be better off to leave the possibility of its reality open and seek out its possible good than to turn away.

There are several other hallmarks of the mystical experience. One is a strong sense of the familiar, no matter how unusual the outer situation. Once I was watching a play. An actor said, "I've returned as I promised." Suddenly, the play opened up. I felt that God spoke through the actor, and I was in tears that God had returned. I've walked in ruined churches that I'd not seen before and suddenly had an overwhelming feeling of the familiar. In the ruins of a monks' abbey, I was suddenly familiar with the monks and their devoted labor of building the church. Sometimes when interviewing a person, it also occurs that, suddenly, again, there is the familiar God in them. The feeling is very pleasant, like coming home after a long trip. It often comes to me when I'm with people talking about sharing with others or about universal humanity. The full mystical experience leaves a very broad signature on the inner life that then finds itself expressed in many ways. The sense of familiarity is so consistent that I would question whether the experience of deja vu might not be a part of mysticism. I would encourage those with deja vu to reflect deeply on what they recognize in the experience. Try to bring up and examine all the feelings. It may be a tiny precursor to the mystical. I was once talking to a neurotic woman. There was something in her very preened formality. Suddenly, I felt the essence of Egyptian religion. It is difficult to describe, but it has to do with reaching and preserving the contact with the Eternal. The changeless is close to the sacred—so it was necessary to preserve the body. A religion that seemed foreign to me was suddenly familiar. It revered the changeless, which is an approach to the Eternal.

There is another aspect of the mystical experience that seems to be consistently misunderstood. It is as though we must die to ourselves in order to see God. This leads to all sorts of efforts to overcome the self. This is an impossible paradox, for the one struggling against the self turns out to be simply the self. In a way, the self is actually intensified by the effort to get rid of it. The truth is that in a mystical experience there is an expansion of the self—quite the opposite. It is as though God is always present and is the root and source of our very life. God need only expand our awareness to come into consciousness. The relaxed openness is part of allowing this to happen, allowing the source to speak. The love of God calls forth the experience.

There is another related problem. I've wondered if I should tell you of my great visions. Readers might compare their little visions to my great ones and conclude that they have not yet reached the same level. This is a kind of spiritual nonsense. Like Swedenborg,[6] we become disappointed if our vision doesn't knock us clear out of bed. It is the doubting little self that demands miracles, lightning to strike this very instant. What is wrong is that this competitive race for the biggest vision overlooks all the tiny ones. It is loving appreciation of the tiny ones that may (God willing) prepare us for a bigger vision. A key to understanding here is that we really can't (repeat, *can't*) make God come give us a giant experience. This is a presumption against the very nature of the spiritual. Learn to appreciate the absolute wonder that you already have. We breathe, don't we? Isn't it a marvelous process that we take in and expel the world regularly, whether we think of it or not? I wonder if there is meaning beyond oxygenating the blood. The Hindus have described a way to God that includes principally focusing on breathing. Earlier I described a mystical experience in simply looking at and wondering at the life that cleverly moves my hands, I know not how. Looking at and enjoying the wonder of nature is a universal experience of humankind. Beware of asking God for big visions, just to prove he exists. Having had one vision, you may tend to doubt it and ask for one more bigger one, and so on. Finally, you will die; and it is hoped that the vision you have then will at last be big enough!

Both the effort to overcome the self and the demand for big visions are common spiritual traps. God comes by expanding your present awareness. Learn to see the miracles here all the time. The very essence of the mystical experience is to appreciate what is here now. That is becoming a child again—finding amazingly beautiful something as small as a dried-up leaf that fell from a tree.

Some may conclude that the mystical can be sensed in the beautiful things in life (i.e., nature) but not in the ugly things. Not so. I have reflected on rubbish and garbage heaps and found wonders in them. Some put a big boundary between the things made by God (i.e., nature) and those made by human beings. In this dichotomy, human creations are low and nature's high. This seems foolish to me. I am so aware that God designed the people who make things, that I am most anxious to watch science's discoveries and the unfolding of clever electronic gadgets. If you look for God, he may be found anywhere.

It would be fair to ask what the mystic ultimately discovers. Swedenborg's writings contain some of the better descriptions.

## Swedenborg's Mysticism

I cannot but open up those things of the Word that are called mystical, that is, its interior things. . . .

(*Arcana Coelestia* 4923)

It came as a considerable surprise to me to learn that there is a tradition among students of Swedenborg's religious writings that Swedenborg is not a mystic. It is only too apparent to a mystic that his works are a major contribution to this literature, and mystics have freely referred to him as one of their own. Swedenborg's spiritual writings define mysticism in a way that inescapably makes Swedenborg a mystic. How is it, then, that some of his followers say, with earnest conviction, that he is not a mystic? We will look at what mysticism precisely is and how this error arose. We will also see how his religious works define mysticism and how this compares with the current accepted meaning. This is not a mere quibble over a term. At its least, it implies a misunderstanding of mysticism. At its worst, it may involve a misunderstanding of the very nature of Swedenborg's writings themselves.

The definition of mysticism has two conflicting currents. One, which we will call the scholarly definition, reflects the actual experience of mystics. The other, which we will call the layperson's definition, stands outside the experience and basically says it doesn't make sense. This confusion of opposing definitions is quite old and extends back before Swedenborg's time. Many dictionaries will reflect both views. The core of the scholarly definitions is the experience of union with the Divine. The core of the layperson's definitions is whatever is occult, mysterious, unclear, or involved with spirits.

Followers who use the layperson's definition are more than happy to say Swedenborg wasn't interested in the occult, which is true, and hence not a mystic. The very rationality and clarity of his spiritual writings would seem to militate against their being mystical. Let us look at the dictionary definitions. The closer the dictionary is to the popular mind, the more likely it will reflect the unprofessional layperson's definition as well as the scholarly. Scholarly religious dictionaries tend to drop the popular misconception altogether and deal only with the real internal meaning of the experience. The following reflects more of the popular misconception:

> Mystical. 1. mystic; occult 2. of or pertaining to mystics or mysticism: mystical writings. 3. spiritually symbolic. 4. rare: obscure in meaning; mysterious.[7]

Swedenborg's own definition was the third one above— "spiritually symbolic." This same dictionary, reflecting the popular conception, says of the word *mystic*: "known only to the initiated; of occult power or significance; of obscure or mysterious character . . ." It is from this aspect that followers of Swedenborg's religious writings wanted to dissociate themselves, for these works are eminently rational and clear. Another dictionary almost overlooks this popular misconception:

> Mystical. 1: having a spiritual meaning or reality, or the like, neither apparent to the senses nor obvious to the intelligence; symbolical; as, the church is the mystical body of Christ. 2: of, resulting from, or manifesting an individual's direct communion with God, through contemplation, vision, an inner light, or the like; as, mystical rapture. 3. now rare: unintelligible; cryptic.[8]

Notice that the definitions "obscure in meaning, mysterious" and "cryptic" are now seen as rare.

It is through communion with the Divine that direct spiritual understanding is given, which is often symbolic and difficult to translate into ordinary terms for others. The difficulty of conveying the internal experience to others has made it seem obscure to outsiders. Then, to add to the confusion, there have been the pseudomystics who use the term for self-aggrandizement, as though to say, "This is mystical and too deep for your understanding, but, of course, I understand it!"

The very authoritative *Hastings Encyclopedia of Religion and Ethics* goes to the heart of the matter:

> Mysticism. "Mysticism," in common speech-usage, is a word of very uncertain connotation. It has in recent times been used as an equivalent for two characteristically different German words: *Mystizismus*, which stands for the cult of the supernatural, for theosophical pursuits, for a spiritualistic exploitation of physical research; and *Mystik*, which stands for immediate experience of a divine-human intercourse and relationship. The word "mysticism" has, furthermore, been commonly used to cover both (1) the first-hand experience of direct intercourse with God and (2) the theologico-metaphysical doctrine of the soul's possible union with Absolute Reality, i.e., with God. It would be conducive to clarity to restrict the word "mysticism" to the latter significance, namely, as an equivalent for the German word *Mystik* and as designating the historic doctrine of the relationship and potential union of the human soul with Ultimate Reality, and to use the term "mystical experience" for direct intercourse with God.
>
> First-hand, or mystical, experience is primarily a psychological question; the doctrine of mysticism is essentially a metaphysical problem. Mystical experience is as old as humanity, is not confined to any one racial

stock, is undoubtedly one of the original grounds of
personal religion, and does not stand or fall with the
truth or falsity of the metaphysically formulated doctrine of mysticism. Mystical experience is marked by
the emergence of a type of consciousness.[9]

The more than twenty pages of tiny print make no further
reference to the layperson's definition. In spite of what
the author, Rufus Jones, a noted scholar of mysticism,
would like to see, the term *mysticism* is used most often for
the experience. The literature on the qualities of the experience is vast; that on the doctrinal aspects is relatively
scant. In, fact Swedenborg's spiritual writings are an unusual combination of the experiential and the doctrinal
aspects of mysticism. In brief, then, the most accepted definition of mysticism refers to all aspects of the experience of conjunction or union with the Divine and,
secondarily, to doctrines about this. This is the sense in
which I use the term.

It is relatively easy to demonstrate that all those who
have said Swedenborg was not a mystic used the now-rare
and not really acceptable layperson's definition. None of
them was trying to say that his writings do not deal with
the experience of the Divine—the core of the accepted
meaning of mysticism. My sources are not complete, but a
couple of references will illustrate the point.

Herbert C. Small in 1929 did one of the more impres-
sive antimystical articles. A few quotes will show he is
using the layperson's definition: "Mysticism is the main
cause of all religious superstition and phantasy. . . . These
experiences run the entire gamut of magic, spiritism, oc-
cultism, Holy Ghostism, theosophy . . . and what not. . . .
[Swedenborg] sought no occult source, and employed

none."[10] Small's complete argument can't be put down so easily. Basically, he says that mystics are led by their own intuition, which becomes an authority higher than the Word. This is simply not true. There are countless mystics who revere the Word because they have experienced something of its inner sense. But his is the view of the one outside the experience. Indeed, he feels those who have the experience are incompetent to judge it; only one outside it can be a proper judge: "It is quite useless in most cases to rely on definitions of mysticism as given by its devotees, for they have no knowledge of its true nature."[11] Standing outside the experience, he links it to all excesses of self leading and falling into occult and mysterious falsities. If, for his use of the term, one substitutes the now-accepted meaning of the term—the experience of the Divine—then all his arguments would fail; for he could not say the one who has no experience of the Divine is better able to judge the worth of the experience than one who *has known* God. There would be no linking to "spiritism," for the experience of God is not the experience of spirits. He emphasized Swedenborg the scientist, collecting and analyzing facts; but he had to admit Swedenborg was led of the Lord, which is precisely what the now-accepted definition of mysticism means.

In a recent example, Brian Kingslake also disclaims Swedenborg as a mystic.[12] Though he finds many similarities between Swedenborg's life and that of other prominent mystics, he sees a difference in that Swedenborg's religious works are rational. Mysticism is nonrational; this is again from the layperson's definition. As a matter of fact, mystical writings vary across the whole spectrum of clarity and rationality. Basically, mysticism, or the experience of God, is irrational to those outside the experience. It is rational, true, and clear to those in the experience. It informs reason of higher truths. If Swedenborg had not clarified his experience beyond the *Spiritual Diary,* he would appear to have been very irrational. The experience of God makes a higher sense. Seen in the whole of the world's mystical literature, Swedenborg's spiritual writings are perhaps near average for clarity or rationality. When you go to the heart of the meaning of mysticism— the experience of God—and substitute this for the word *mysticism,* then most of the arguments that Swedenborg was no mystic fall. He obviously had much experience of God and tried to teach us of this, which is precisely what being a mystic means. Some will find it clear and rational, and others will not. The closer one is to a similar experience of the Divine, the clearer and more rational these works of Swedenborg will seem. For example, by comparison, Christ's teachings are perhaps even clearer and much of Böhme's works less clear.

The only perceptive use of mysticism I was able to find in the collateral literature was in Marguerite Block's conclusion to her historical survey. Two quotes might entice some readers to review the whole chapter:

> The New Church in general has ignored the mystical side of religion, though it is absolutely inherent in the doctrine of influx—the entrance of God into the individual soul, as well as in the doctrine of perception, or interior reception of spiritual truth.[13]

> Perhaps after all the issue in the New Church is not the simple and obvious one between "fundamentalism" and "modernism," but the more ancient one between

literalism and mysticism which has appeared in almost
all the world's religions at various times.[14]

I suspect Block has her finger on the difficulty. I fear that
there are natural and fundamentally different approaches
to reality and human experience reflected in her literalism versus mysticism, that, even if Swedenborg were a classic mystic, the literalists would not be able to discover this.
But this is another whole large issue, whether any amount
of doctrine can ever get us to break out of the shell of our
inherent approach to reality.

The following will clarify the contrasting definitions of
mysticism:

## MYSTICISM

| *The outsider's position, layperson's rare meaning* | *The inside experience, scholarly accepted definition* |
|---|---|
| Being led by every emotional whim | Being led by God |
| Concerned with spirits and other powers | Concerned with God alone |
| Irrational and mysterious | Rational, a higher under-standing |
| Seen as contrary to the authority of Swedenborg's religious writings | Seen as reinforcing the authority of Swedenborg's religious writings |
| Each is a law unto himself | God rules all |

What do Swedenborg's religious writings themselves say
of mysticism? It is disturbing to me to think of all those
who claim to stand on the authority of his writings and

choose to overlook what they say of mysticism. Swedenborg uses the term "mystical" (*mysticus*) rarely, only fourteen times that I count in his work. In the Latin, it means what is hidden or secret. He uses it in several related senses, which include both the layperson's and the scholarly uses.

Sometimes he uses it to disparage the pretentiously obscure (*Arcana Coelestia* 5223, 7296) or the irrational, such as the mystic dogma of the trinity (*True Christian Religion* 169) or when he refers to the mystical and enigmatical faith of present-day theology (*True Christian Religion* 351).

At other times, he uses it to mean the sacred that is not understood and appreciated and, hence, rejected. Speaking of the science of representations and correspondences, which is often rejected, he writes:

> Hardly anyone is willing to believe that it exists, and
> they who do believe this, merely called it something
> mystical that is of no use.
>
> > (*Arcana Coelestia* 2763)

> And if what is internal or spiritual is merely men
> tioned, they either ridicule it or call it mystical; conse
> quently, all conjunction between them is broken, and
> when this is broken, the spiritual man suffers griev
> ously among the merely natural.
>
> > (*Arcana Coelestia* 5022)

> But what is meant thereby, Christianity (now-a-days)
> does not enquire because it places the celestial and
> spiritual things of the Word in its literal sense, and calls
> its interior things mystical for which it does not care.
>
> > (*Arcana Coelestia* 9688)

But these are his peripheral uses of the word *mystical.* In his strongest and most unambiguous uses, he refers to the interior spiritual and celestial sense of the Word. Note the power of these statements:

> I cannot but open up to those things of the Word that are called mystical, that is, its interior things, which are the spiritual and celestial things of the Lord's kingdom.
>
> *(Arcana Coelestia* 4923)

> The mystical things which some seek in the Word, are nothing else than the spiritual and celestial senses.
>
> *(The Word of the Lord from Experience* 21)

> The arcana of wisdom of the three heavens contained in [the Word] are the mystical things of which many have spoken.
>
> *(Apocalypse Explained* 1079)

> "I am in the Father, and the Father in Me." This is the mystical union of which many speak.
>
> *(Arcana Coelestia* 2004)

Paragraph 4923 of *Arcana Coelestia* is worth reading in its entirety. Very clearly Swedenborg says the holy and the mystical that many felt existed in the Word, and for which they search, is nothing other than the interior of the Word, which he describes.

Does Swedenborg's definition of the mystical as the internal of the Word accord with the present-day scholarly definition? It is fully in accord if you are careful of what is meant. If one said "the experience of the internal sense," then there would be no doubt. The internal of the Word is the life of God. Experience of this internal sense is the experience of the Divine. I make this proviso so that one does not mistakenly think a mere knowledge of this internal sense brings one into the spiritual and celestial, which is the internal of the Bible. Some kind of living involvement in the internal sense is necessary, and involvement that leads to uses and charity. To me, one of my more significant discoveries was the way Swedenborg personally invested himself in his study of the Bible.[15] This went beyond "knowledge of" to entering into the "life of" the internal. If one is thinking of a living participation in the internal sense of the Word, then Swedenborg's definition of the mystical accords with the modern scholarly meaning of mysticism. Can we then say that the person who "cannot but open up those things of the Word that are called mystical" is not a mystic?

There is a larger sense in which Swedenborg was clearly a mystic, a sense that breaks out of the limitations of a single word he actually didn't use very often. In the accepted positive scholarly sense, the mystic is simply one who has direct experience of the Divine. I doubt that any follower of Swedenborg's spiritual writings would say Swedenborg did not have direct experience of the Divine. Then, he *was* a mystic. Mystics who write attempt to share their experience and its subsequent understandings with others. Contrary to the ideas of some that mysticism is irrational, most mystics who have written have produced quite rational works. In only a few places did Swedenborg say it was more than could be told or that it was not permitted yet to reveal. He made an eminent attempt to convey his direct experience and his consequent understandings. Have other mystics attempted to make as clear or rational a presentation? Indeed, yes. To those who want to pursue

further the positive side of mysticism, I recommend the
works of Evelyn Underhill, especially her *Practical Mysticism*.[16] Her big volume *Mysticism*[17] leads one to the larger
body of world literature on the subject.

Is there more mysticism in Swedenborg's religious writings than one man sharing his experience and findings of
the Divine? I believe so, but this point cannot be proven
in a limited space. If the mysticism of his writing lies preeminently in the internal sense of the Word, why is this
sense presented to us? Is it to satisfy our curiosity, so we by-
standers can look in at the dynamics of the life of God? I
don't believe this is its purpose at all. Instead, I submit
that this was presented so we might come into the kingdom. If I had to describe Swedenborg's spiritual writings
and their fundamental purpose in one line, it would be
this: the writings are a clear presentation meant to be
used by individuals to lead them into the life of God—as
an actual part of their experience. His writings are rational, but that is their style, not preeminently their nature.
Their nature and overwhelming purpose are to lead to
God, which accounts for many aspects of their structure.
So in this sense, not only are his writings the work of a
mystic, they are meant to help create mystics, that is, to
lead others to the Divine. I am quite in accord with the
position of some regarding the sacredness and authority
of Swedenborg's writings.

Perhaps a few words on the general nature of mysticism
in organized religion may help those to whom the connection of mysticism and Swedenborg's religious writings
is new. Mystics, those who have contact with the Divine,
have sprung up in all religions, all cultures, and all times.
They express themselves variously in the forms and uses

of their time, culture, and religion. Contrary to the outsider's idea that they may depart on any wild whim or intuition, persons with the experience of the Divine tend to be able to recognize this in others even across the barriers of time and circumstances. It is as though, having touched the universal, they can recognize others who have also done so. They tend to be socially useful; and, in fact, their uses may be the only outer expression of their experience of the Divine. Like Swedenborg, they tend to support the old religious forms but give them deeper meaning. It is not appropriate to rank them as to which is the greater mystic, for they are in no contest with each other. Rather we can say, "This one touches me and that one doesn't," which describes our own uniqueness. It is characteristic of mystics that they speak from experience rather than from speculation and past authority. It is often their lot to be seen as a threat to conventional religious authority, which may not dare claim an experience of God. Are mystics rare? Not really. Probably all persons have the experience of the Divine, often in childhood, but people differ in how conscious and ruling this experience is. Included in the scholarly definition is nature mysticism—the feeling of God present in nature—which must be a universal experience.

What is the evidence in Swedenborg's writings that he came into the experience of God? There is an even more critical interior question: what in his writings can lead you to God? To a mystic the signs of Swedenborg's contact with God are too legion to catalog, but I'll deal with the most general first. Throughout his writings, Swedenborg is saying, "I have experienced . . ." This is not said in an aggrandizing way. The whole *Spiritual Diary* contains his experiences. The "memorable relations" scattered through all of his religious writings are experiences. He makes practically no reference to other scholars or theologians. On a few occasions, he says the internal sense of the Bible was revealed by the Lord alone. No angels or spirits led him in this. Does he mean the Lord dictated the *Arcana Coelestia* word for word? I don't believe so. It was a noetic, direct-knowing experience. The experience has very pleasant inner verities, so one knows beyond doubt the real author. I am reminded of the phrase somewhere in the Bible that the sheep know their master. I picture a shepherd who lives all day with his sheep and sleeps with them at night. They know his very footsteps and smell. It is that kind of interior familiarity that exists in Swedenborg's writing.

Secondly, his writings not only come from experience but their real substance deals primarily with *human* experience. It is not as though the Divine and the human are two contents; there is but one content: the Divine/human. Swedenborg's is an immensely human view of theology. This may not be apparent to everyone. *Heaven and Hell* deals with angels, spirits, and demons. If they are human, don't they at least seem a bit removed from our world of humans? Not so. We have each experienced something of heaven and hell in this world. While we are in this life, we each participate in societies of heaven and hell. That is, by our very nature, choices, or uses, we are intimately related to aspects of heaven and hell. Moreover, I am struck how heaven and hell can also be understood as deeper aspects of mind. We not only exist by influx through the spiritual worlds, but also our interior design is in their form. For me, it has been a useful clarification to think how acts of mine and others may be heavenly or hellish.

The interior human aspect is throughout his writings. "Evidently it is these delights that rule the man's thoughts, and the thoughts are nothing apart from them; yet they seem to him to be nothing but thoughts; when, in fact, thoughts are nothing but affections so composed into forms by his life's love as to be presented in light" (*Divine Providence* 199). It took a good deal of close observation to see that thoughts are formed of affections or feelings. The whole of the twelve-volume *Arcana Coelestia* has to do with the Lord's glorification, which is the model for the individual's spiritual development. But Swedenborg isn't merely dealing with the psychology of persons. His is a unique psychology thoroughly pervaded and informed by his spiritual experience. In two words, it is a *spiritual psychology*. Because he is dealing with the very stuff of human existence, what he has to say is ultimately open to empirical test. I don't quite mean it is open to scientific test because science can only deal with what is external. But I do mean it is open to test and confirmation by individuals. My pamphlet on *Uses*[18] is an example of bringing one of Swedenborg's core doctrines into personal experience, where the individual can see for oneself if it is true.

How is it that a boy's early experiences of wonder could eventually teach him to respect Swedenborg? For me, the whole of religion is like a single tree. Religions are branches and the sects are leaves. We can concentrate on the leaves—how this one is different from that one, this finer than that. Or we can look to the one life of the tree. If we concentrate on differences, the whole is impossibly complex and confusing. As a boy, and now as a man, I badly need to understand the one life of the tree. This brings me the peace of heaven. I find myself in profound accord with a man born three centuries ago, a man who walked in silver buckled shoes and me in Adidas sneakers. He put words to what used to be nameless for me:

> Hence it is plain that the church of the Lord is not here, nor there, but that it is everywhere, both within those kingdoms where the church is, and outside them, where men live according to the precepts of charity. Hence it is that the church of the Lord is scattered through the whole world, and yet it is one; for when life makes the church and not doctrine separate them from life, then the church is one, but when doctrine makes the church, then there are many.
>
> (*Arcana Coelestia* 8152)

I have difficulty in answering the question of what religion I belong to. If the questioner is reflective, I answer with surprise, "Do you honestly mean there is more than one?" But to others, I answer simply, "I belong to all religions."

Some will think it must be a life of constant highs to be a mystic. Not so. Much of the time I grumble at my fate and God kicks me. It is sometimes that way with lovers. But it is a respite to wander among Swedenborg's words, touched here and there, and shot through with a wonderful light.

## Notes

1. Thomas Troward, *Edinburgh Lectures in Mental Science* (New York: Dodd, Mead, 1909).
2. Ibid., p. 50.

3. Ibid., p. 54.

4. Raymond Moody, *Life After Life* (Atlanta, GA: Mockingbird Books, 1975).

5. William James, *The Varieties of Religious Experience* (New York: Modern Library, 1902), p. 371.

6. Wilson Van Dusen, *Swedenborg's Journal of Dreams* (New York: Swedenborg Foundation, 1986).

7. *Random House Dictionary of the English Language* (New York: Random House, 1966).

8. *Webster's Collegiate Dictionary* (Springfield, MA: Merriman, 1942).

9. *Hastings Encyclopedia of Religion and Ethics* (New York: Scribners, 1961)

10. Herbert Small, "What Is a Mystic?" *The Messenger* (1929): 340.

11. Ibid.

12. Brian Kingslake, "Was Swedenborg a Mystic?" *New Church Magazine* (1977): 52ff.

13. Marguerite Block, *The New Church in the New World* (New York: Octagon, 1968), p. 393.

14. Ibid., p. 400.

15. Wilson Van Dusen, "Another Key to Swedenborg's Development," *New Church Life* (1975): 316–319.

16. Evelyn Underhill, *Practical Mysticism* (New York: Dutton, 1915).

17. Evelyn Underhill, *Mysticism* (New York: Dutton, 1961).

18. Wilson Van Dusen, *Uses* (New York: Swedenborg Foundation, 1978; rpt. 1987).

EUGENE TAYLOR

# Emerson: The Swedenborgian and Transcendentalist Connection

## BY EUGENE TAYLOR

Ralph Waldo Emerson, son of a long line of New England preachers, was born in a parsonage in Boston, 1803, and grew up in an urban setting still rural enough to walk his mother's cow each morning to graze on the Boston Common. Emerson's father, the Reverend William Emerson, although not well off, was a force in the local intellectual community as a founder of the Boston Athenaeum, member of the Massachusetts Historical Society, and participant in the Physiological Society at the home of Dr. James Jackson. He died in 1811, leaving Mrs. Emerson and her six children bereft of financial support. Despite these limitations, Waldo, as he was then called, successfully passed through Boston Latin School; and, with the help of his grandfather, the Reverend Ezra Ripley of Concord, entered Harvard College in 1817. Not so well off as the other students, Emerson had to wait tables in the student dining hall, and he had the added duty of "President's Freshman," a position in which he was

responsible for communicating messages from President
Kirkland to the first-year students. Emerson was also required to call those duly summoned for infractions. In
exchange for these tasks, he received his meals and lodg-
ing in the form of a room over President Kirkland's
study.[1]

While time-consuming, these activities put Emerson in
contact with every member of his class, and he was soon
known throughout the college. Not yet having decided
upon a definite vocation, he pursued the regular course
of studies but in a somewhat lackluster fashion. His biographers tell us that he liked to spend most of his time
thinking, taking walks, and composing poetry. Oliver
Wendell Holmes's brother John later remembered Emerson as quiet, unobtrusive, only a fair scholar, but every
inch a king in his dominion.

During Emerson's freshman year, a Swedenborgian
study group flourished among a few Harvard students
who were his acquaintances and who were destined to
play a role in providing what was perhaps the first literary
impulse to Emerson's career. Chief among these were
Sampson Reed and Thomas Worcester. Reed, born in
Bridgewater, Massachusetts, June 10, 1800, son of the Reverend John Reed, was raised on his father's farm and entered Harvard in 1814. During his first year at college, he
met Thomas Worcester because Reed's father was a mutual friend of the Reverend Pitt Clark, to whom Worcester
had previously been apprenticed. As freshmen, Worcester
and Reed occupied rooms in the same private residence
near President Kirkland's house, and they became college
roommates the following year, despite a difference in

ages—Worcester was nineteen and Reed, five years his junior. Both were impoverished students and most of their expenses were paid by waiting tables at the dining hall, which, by their senior year, put them in contact with Emerson, also working at the same occupation. Like Emerson, they, too, taught school during the winter vacation in order to make ends meet.[2]

Reed was most diligent in his college studies, while Worcester's principal activity was in reading Swedenborg's *Heavenly Doctrines*[3] and in transmitting their content to his fellow Harvard students. A set of Swedenborg's writings had been deposited in the college library in 1794 by the Reverend William Hill, and Worcester had contrived by ingenious means to get his hands on the complete collection. He kept these volumes on his mantel with the permission of President Kirkland for the four years he was a student, and his room quickly became the center of many student discussions and conferences. In addition to Sampson Reed, this circle included Thomas B. Hayward, John H. Wilkins, Nathaniel Hobart, Caleb Reed, Warren Goddard, and Theophilus Parsons. Reed and Worcester graduated in the class of 1818, when Emerson was beginning his sophomore year. Both immediately enrolled in the theological school, which at that time had not yet attained an independent status from the college. One merely stayed on in the capacity of what was called a "Resident Graduate," to read for the ministry.

At this same time, the nucleus of the first Boston Swedenborgian Society was formed in Cambridge at the boardinghouse of Mrs. Thomazine E. Minot, who had set up housekeeping in hopes of furthering the work of the church among Harvard students. Worcester, Reed, and others found it a congenial home and religious center while pursuing their ministerial studies. Other interested persons also gathered there to read Swedenborg's works; and, out of these meetings, twelve people constituted the original founding body of the First Swedenborgian Church in Boston, still situated downtown on Bowdoin Street. In 1821, this society officially asked Thomas Worcester to become its pastor, and he accepted. Worcester married that same year; and Mrs. Minot, seeing that her work in Cambridge had come to an end, moved her home to Boston, which then provided living facilities for the new parson and his new wife. Sampson Reed and his classmate, John H. Wilkins, left their theological studies to join the activities of the new church. Reed became a teacher for a short time, while Wilkins published a small book on astronomy, the success of which soon led him into the book business.

In August 1821, Reed received a Master of Arts degree at Harvard and, at the same time, delivered a speech at the commencement ceremonies entitled "Oration on Genius." Emerson, just completing his Bachelor of Arts degree, participated in the ceremony as Class Day Poet—after seven before him had declined the invitation. He was present in the audience when Reed gave his oration and was greatly pleased by the speech. The commencement audience found it tedious because, as one auditor put it, it was so "miserably delivered"; but Emerson later referred to it as "native gold" and, after the presentation, prevailed upon his brother William, who was in Reed's class, to borrow the manuscript. Emerson "copied the whole of it and kept it as a treasure."[4] He referred to the work frequently in his journals, and the oration was passed around and discussed freely among Emerson's family.[5] As Perry Miller has described it,

> It was the first admonitory indictment of formalism in the liberal church and pointed the way for an appeal from institutional legalities to a fresh and creative approach to nature; it insinuated that the first requirement would be a rejection of Locke. And then it took as its subject "genius"—with the implication that all who turned to nature could be geniuses. It excited the expectation of a new day, and it did so in an oracular, cryptic style, such as had not been heard in New England before, no accent of which was lost on the delighted eighteen-year-old Waldo Emerson.[6]

Love, Reed said in this oration, is the very life of man. The brute depends on physical strength, while the great man depends on society, particularly the state of its arts and sciences. But the spiritual man knows that love and wisdom are from no other source than the Divine. Great men are not more like God than others. But because we believe the opposite, we fall into worshiping other men, rather than the Divine. Divinity shines through man. When we see this, we should rejoice in the truth itself and not rejoice in the mere fact that we have found it. There is an ambition that hurries a man after truth and takes away the power of attaining it. Genius in this regard may carry the seed of its own destruction. Genius is divine not when man thinks he is God but when he sees his powers are from God. So it is true of the arts, for feelings of all kinds will discover themselves in music, in painting, in poetry; but it is only when the heart is purified from every selfish and worldly passion that they are created in real beauty, for in their origin they too are Divine.

Science, Reed continued, is more fixed; its laws according to which natural things are fixed are either true or false. Because God is love, nature exists. Science becomes sterile without according nature its true divine origin. After all, man may see the light, but he does not make it. In nature, both the sciences and the arts exist embodied. Only when the heart is purified from all selfishness and worldly affections will the genius of the mind descend to unite with all nature. Only then will a new age of science dawn as surely as we ask, "Watchman, what of the night?" and he says, "The morning cometh."[7]

"Oration on Genius" was a remarkable spiritual document that would later become the basis for Reed's *Growth of the Mind* (1826). But by 1822, his finances strained, Reed turned from teacher to apothecary's apprentice, and this finally became his principal trade. That same year, Emerson entered the theology school; and, while not enrolled as a regular student, he began studying under William Ellery Channing. The impression is left that Emerson continued to pursue his own interests. We hear, for instance, that because his eyes had troubled him, he had not taken notes for his lectures and so was excused from examinations. He had begun keeping his journals the year before; and in December 1824, he made his first reference to the Swedenborgians, classifying them as a quiet little sect like the Quakers.[8]

After three years of independent study, Emerson was approbated to preach by the Middlesex Association of

Ministers. He later said of this rite of passage, "If they had examined me they probably would not let me preach at all."[9] Meanwhile, by 1825, Sampson Reed had opened his own wholesale drug business on Hanover Street, taken an assistant, and immediately found time to write. He prepared a short article based on his 1821 oration for the *North American Review,* which the editor recommended be published as a book. The article was praised by one reader as "some essential poetry of high order." It was duly enlarged and published in August 1826, under the title *Growth of the Mind,* brought out by the book company of his classmate John H. Wilkins.[10]

Emerson's reading of Reed confirmed the doctrine of self-reliance, the reality of the World Spirit, and the feebleness of the arts and sciences when divorced from their true source. From the work, Emerson also confirmed the importance of the genuine man, as opposed to the merely great man; and he saw in it both the harmony of philosophy and religion and a nearly unshakable optimism in the future. And as we shall see in his own book *Nature,* foremost was the Swedenborgian idea of correspondences.

On September 10, 1826, Emerson hailed Reed's little book as a "revelation."[11] Three days later, he wrote to his brother William that it was one of the best books he had ever seen.[12] On September 29, he again wrote to his brother mentioning Reed's book, saying that it was a rich work, comparable to Plato, and that its author should have the chair of philosophy then recently vacated at Harvard by Professor Levi Frisbie. Emerson was amused, however, that this great work had been composed in a drugstore.[13]

He lost no time in sending a copy to Aunt Mary Moody Emerson. He wrote to her, "Has any modern hand touched the harp of great nature so rarely? Has any looked so shrewdly into the subtle and concealed connection of man and nature, of heaven and earth"?[14] Aunt Mary's response to the book was that she found in it "triteness, obscurity," and "Swedenishness." And she thought its rarer parts were culled from Wordsworth, who was no Swedenborg.[15]

Nevertheless, Reed's ideas entered into Emerson's sermons and journal passages with renewed vigor. In 1827, for instance, Emerson wrote "Peculiarities of the Present Age." Under "Transcendentalism," he listed Reed as the best American representative and Swedenborg as the best "from Germany" (*sic*).[16] This, by the way, was Emerson's first use of the word *transcendentalism* in his journals. He referred to Reed as a spiritual rather than secular teacher, and he regarded him as one of a number of personal acquaintances who had enriched his life. His journals into the 1830s recount several conversations with Reed and Worcester.[17] By 1827, Reed had helped launch a new magazine, *The Swedenborgian Messenger*; and, from further references in his journals, it is evident that Emerson examined succeeding issues of this publication and read Reed's many articles. In 1832, for instance, Emerson quoted Swedenborg, who "considered the visible world and the relation of its parts as the dial plate of the invisible one."[18] Was this the origin of the name for the later transcendentalist publication *The Dial*?

In the latter part of 1833, Emerson returned from his first European trip. It was an uncertain time for him, as he had then recently lost both his first wife and his brother and resigned his pulpit in Boston after his congregation had refused to allow him to give up administering communion, which, he said, he no longer believed in. He lived first in Boston, then in Newton during this period.

For money, he turned to public speaking. To his surprise, he found, upon mounting the public lecture platform, that he could get people to listen to religious subjects on Wednesday evening to which their ears were absolutely closed on Sunday morning. Curiously enough, his first lectures as a secular prophet were on scientific topics before the Boston Society for Natural History. He did not give up preaching entirely, however. At one point, he traveled to New Bedford to deliver a guest sermon and recorded in his journals with pleasure the comment of a Swedenborgian minister friend, Dr. Artemas Stebbins, who said that he felt excused from preaching while Emerson was in the vicinity because the people were receiving from him as much of the New Church doctrine as they could bear.[19]

On May 14, 1834, Emerson first wrote to his new friend Thomas Carlyle. With his letter, he sent a volume of [Daniel] Webster's speeches, which Emerson included "with a little book of my Swedenborgian druggist, of whom I told you."[20] It was, of course, *Growth of the Mind.* Carlyle replied on August 12, "I have read both your books at leisure times, and now nearly finished the smaller one. He is a faithful thinker, that Swedenborgian Druggist of yours, with really deep ideas, who makes me pause and think, were it only to consider what manner of man *he* must be. 'Through the smallest window look well, and you can look out into the infinite.' "[21] Emerson responded on November 20, 1834: "I am glad you like

Sampson Reed, and that he has inspired some curiosity respecting his church. Swedenborgianism, if you should be fortunate in your first meetings, has many points of attraction for you."[22] He went on to mention the natural world as a symbol of the spiritual, the animals as incarnations of certain affections, and the use of all figurative language as statements of spiritual fact. The Swedenborgian theory of social relations, Emerson wrote, was most philosophical and, while at variance with popular theology, self-evident. Emerson objected to the descriptive theism of the Swedenborgians, to the accounts of what he called "their drollest heaven," and to certain of their autocratic decrees of God. "In general too," he said, "they receive the fable instead of the moral of their Aesop. They are to me, however, deeply interesting, as a sect which I think must contribute more than all other sects to the new faith which must arise out of all."[23]

Emerson, then, introduced Carlyle to Swedenborg through Reed's work. Evidence for this comes from a letter Carlyle wrote, August 2, 1838, to Dr. James John Garth Wilkinson, English physician and translator of Swedenborg's pretheological writings. Wilkinson asked Carlyle if he had read Swedenborg, to which Carlyle replied:

Hitherto I have known nearly nothing of Swedenborg; or indeed, I might say less than nothing, having been wont to picture him as an amiable but insane visionary, with affections quite out of proportion to his insight; from whom nothing at all was to be learned. It is so we judge of extraordinary men. But I have been rebuked already. A little book, by one Sampson Reed, of Boston, in New England, which some friend [Emerson] sent hither, taught me that a Swedenborgian might have thoughts of the calmest kind on the deepest things; that, in short, I did *not* know Swedenborg, and ought to be ready to know him.[24]

This was the beginning of an important relationship between Carlyle and Wilkinson, which would eventually lead Wilkinson into a friendship with Emerson himself.

Emerson, meanwhile, in his journals recorded that, on January 6, 1835, he visited the Swedenborgian Chapel for the first time. He later told Reed, "The sermon was in its style severely simple and in method and manner [was] much [like] a problem in geometry, wholly uncolored and impassioned. . . . With the exception of one passage [it] might have been preached without exciting surprise in any church."[25]

In late February 1836, while preparing the last two chapters of *Nature*, Emerson referred to Reed in his journals as "my early oracle" and again quoted from Reed's "Oration on Genius." He wrote to his brother William, on June 28: "My little book is nearly done. Its title is 'Nature.' Its contents will not exceed in bulk Sampson Reed's 'Growth of the Mind.' My design is to follow it with another essay, 'Spirit,' and the two shall make a decent volume."[26]

In early September 1836, *Nature* appeared anonymously. There are mixed accounts of its sales, but all agree that 500 copies were produced. One account said they were all gone in a month. Before the second American edition appeared in 1849, there were at least six unauthorized pirate editions printed in Great Britain. Up to 1844, some 5,000 to 6,000 of these had been sold. Francis

Bowen at Harvard called it "a contradiction." Oliver Wendell Holmes said that "certain passages . . . [were] as exalted as the language of one who is just coming to himself after having been etherized."[27] It gave Carlyle "true satisfaction"; he called it "the foundation and ground-plan." Bronson Alcott said it was "a gem throughout."[28]

Emerson's main theme, of course, was that the highest use of nature is to draw forth the latent energies of the soul and lead men away from self-love. This, you may remember, was Swedenborg's definition of correspondence. Listen to these passages from *Nature*:

> Before Nature, all mean egotism vanishes. I become a transparent eyeball. . . . The currents of universal being circulate through me. . . .

> When a thinker, resolute to detach every object from personal relations, and see it in the light of thought, shall, at the same time kindle science with the holiest of affections, then will God go forth anew. . . .

> If the Reason be stimulated to more earnest vision, outlines and surfaces become transparent, and are no longer seen; causes and spirits are seen through them. The best moments of life are these delicious awakenings of the higher powers, and the reverential withdrawing of Nature before its God. . . .

> The moral influence of Nature upon every individual is that amount of truth which it illustrates to him. This is the unspeakable but intelligible and practicable meaning of the world conveyed to man, the immortal pupil, in every object of sense. To this one end of Discipline all parts of nature conspire.[29]

This was no literal interpretation of Swedenborg, however, for Emerson rejected as too absolute the so-called Swedenborgian dictionary of correspondences, which required the reader to accept as gospel the exact spiritual meaning Swedenborg himself had placed on each object in nature. Rather, Emerson preferred to adopt the general law to his personal purposes; and, as later commentators have shown, he never tired of collecting specific instances of his own.[30]

In this, we see the seeds of what was soon to become a dark cloud forming in the relation between Reed and Emerson. On October 29, 1836, Emerson wrote again in his journals:

> I have always distinguished Sampson Reed's Oration
> on Genius, and Collin's Ode on the Passions, and all of
> Shakespeare as being works of genius, inasmuch as I
> read them with extreme pleasure and see no clue to
> guide me to their origin, whilst Moore's poetry or
> Scott's was much more comprehensible a subject to
> me. But as I become more acquainted with Sampson
> Reed's books and lectures, the miracle is somewhat
> lessened in the same manner as I once found Burke's
> was. As we advance, shall every man of genius turn to
> us the axis of his mind, then shall he be transparent,
> retaining, however, always the prerogative of an origi-
> nal [thinker].[31]

The rift between Reed and Emerson over their different interpretations of Swedenborg became evident when, in 1838, Reed brought out a new edition of *Growth of the Mind.* In a preface, he flatly called the transcendentalists

unoriginal and parasitic for their appropriation and distortion of Swedenborgian ideas. Emerson retaliated
shortly thereafter by confiding in his journals that it was
not impossible for him to know "SR" because he had become "entrenched *in another Man's mind*" (emphasis
Emerson's). He wrote, "You feel as if you had conversed
with a spy . . . and you have not the satisfaction of a good
deliverance yourself because of the malign influences of
this immense arrogancy and subtle bigotry of his
church."[32]

Nevertheless, Emerson continued to mention Swedenborg favorably in public; in his Phi Beta Kappa address on
the American scholar in 1837 and in his Harvard Divinity
School address in 1838, for instance; and despite their con-
troversy, Reed's work was given an honored place among
the transcendentalists when Elizabeth Peabody published
the "Oration on Genius" in her *Aesthetic Papers* in 1849,
along with articles by Henry David Thoreau, Emerson,
Bronson Alcott, and James John Garth Wilkinson.

Then, in 1842, an entirely new chapter opened in
Emerson's relation to Swedenborgian ideas when he met
the eccentric philosopher of religion, Henry James, Sr., in
New York City. The occasion was a public lecture that
Emerson gave in March of that year. Henry James, Sr., has
left us a vivid picture of that first impression:

> His demeanor upon the platform . . . was modesty it-
> self; not the mere absence of display, but the presence
> of a positive personal grace. His deferential entrance
> upon the scene, his look of inquiry at the desk and the
> chair, his resolute rummaging among his embarrassed

papers, the air of sudden recollection with which he
would suddenly plunge into his pockets for what he
must have known had never been put there, his uncertainty and irresolution as he rose to speak, his deep re-
lieved inspiration as he got well from under the burning glass of his auditor's eyes, and addressed himself at
length to their docile ears instead: no maiden ever appealed more potently to your enamoured and admiring sympathy. And then when he looked over the
heads of his audience into the dim mysterious distance, his weird monotone began to reverberate in
your bosom's depths, and his words flowed on, now
with a river's volume, grand, majestic, free, and anon
diminished themselves to the fitful cadence of a brook,
impeded in its course, and returning in melodious co-
quetry upon itself, and you saw the clear eye eloquent
with nature's purity, and beheld the musing counte-
nance turned within, as it were, and harkening to the
rumor of a far-off but oncoming world: how intensely
personal, how exquisitely characteristic it all was![33]

Earnestly believing Emerson to be a man like himself,
one who sought the inner reality of things, James the
Elder went home after that first night and immediately
wrote to Emerson, extending to him an invitation "to
share in his love of truth." James recounted in his letter
something of his own lonely search and, after pouring
out his soul, said, "You have become a sort of confidant
between me and myself . . . in a manner bound to pro-
mote harmony there."[34] He wrote that he felt he may
have overstepped his bounds in expressing himself so

RALPH WALDO EMERSON

confidently but felt sure Emerson's cordial response would vindicate him.

Emerson accepted the invitation. On his first visit, he met the little babe William, "the young philosopher-to-be," as James called him. Emerson gave the famous blessing over William's crib, which officially, in the lore of the James's family, made Emerson William's godfather. Thereafter, Emerson and James, Sr., launched correspondence and visits that went on for forty years, while Emerson established important relationships with James's children as well.

Just after they first met, James, Sr., helped arrange lectures for Emerson in the New York area, and Emerson always stayed with the James family in what came to be known as "Emerson's room." The lecture circuit, Emerson said, mortified his delicate constitution; and he wrote in his journals that it would "soon become intolerable if it were not for a few friends, who, like women, tempered the acrid mass. Henry James Senior," Emerson wrote, "was a true comfort,—wise, gentle, polished, with heroic manners, and a serenity like the sun."[35] Henry, Jr. the novelist, later in his life recalled one of these visits, where he saw in his mind "the winter firelight of our back parlor at dusk and the great Emerson—I knew he was great, greater than any of our friends—sitting in between my parents . . . as an apparition, sinuously, and I held, elegantly slim, benevolently alien, to any we heard round about."[36]

And what did Henry James, the Elder, see in Emerson? He anticipated from the very first that Emerson was the living embodiment of the Divine Natural Humanity—the perfect man, completely lacking in egotism and sin. But after their first meeting, James was sorely disappointed in his expectations. He quickly discovered that Emerson had no idea how he had gotten the way he was and had no well-worked-out logical system for achieving such a condition, as he knew of it only intuitively. Moreover, Emerson was functionally incapable of entering into any argument or debate about his philosophy, thus robbing James of the most pregnant opportunity for refutation and verification. "Oh Emerson," he once wrote, "you man without a handle"; and another letter began with, "Dear invisible Emerson; Henceforth I commit the visible Emerson to my wife for her repose—and mine in leisure hours . . . but it is to the real, the hidden Emerson that I now write."[37] But to no avail. Emerson's letters made no reply to James's plea for an intellectual system. Emerson only acknowledged the admiration he personally felt because James was so interested in his work.

Despite this slight anamoly in their relationship, Emerson was quite eager to introduce James, Sr., to all his friends. He sent a letter to James by way of Henry David Thoreau, asking for some contribution to *The Dial.* Thoreau returned with a good impression saying, "He is a man and takes his own way, or stands still in his own place. I know of no one so patient to have the good of you. . . . He actually reproaches you by his respect for your poor words. I had three hours' solid talk with him, and he asks me to make free use of his home."[38] Margaret Fuller came to visit just before the Jameses left for England. James thought of her as a "dear and noble woman." Theodore Parker was a frequent guest, and so was Bronson Alcott. Alcott and James had personalities and philosophies that made them simultaneously attractive and repulsive to each other. Unable to tolerate James's translation of Alcott's own idealism into common sense or James's constant attacks on the pretensions of civilized morality, Alcott at one time called James "a sinner to all eternity . . . , damaged goods." James, thinking Alcott had left out the practical application of ideas and that he was a man of understanding who lacked will, called Alcott "an egg, half hatched."[39]

Henry James, Sr., in turn, fueled the transcendentalist fires with ideas from the local social reformers, among them his friends Horace Greeley and Albert Brisbane, two of America's foremost spokesmen for the utopian ideas of Charles Fourier. It was Greeley and Brisbane, we learn from the Emerson biography by Gay Wilson Allen, who first introduced James the Elder to Emerson.[40] James was a member and financial backer of the local Fourierist Association, and his cousin Edmund Tweedy was the official treasurer. We know that Fourierist ideas were of interest to the transcendentalists, as they appeared in essays throughout the pages of *The Dial.*

In 1844, with his wife and two newborn sons, William and Henry, who were a year in age apart, Henry James, Sr., made plans to sail for England. On the eve of his departure, Emerson wrote: "I hear of your plans of traveling with a kind of selfish alarm, as we do the engagement of beautiful women who shall now shine no more on us. We talked along so comfortably together, and the madness (is it?) you find in my logic made such good antagonism, that New York looked greatly nearer and warmer to me for your inhabitation."[41]

When Henry James, Sr., set sail with his family, he went armed with letters from Emerson to Thomas Carlyle and John Sterling. James was immediately admitted to Carlyle's English literary circle, which included John Stuart Mill, Alfred Lord Tennyson, George Lewes, Frederick

Denison Maurice (noted clergyman and Christian socialist of the Church of England), Alexander Bain, and, later, James John Garth Wilkinson.

Before he was there many months, ensconced in suitable accommodations with his family, and while sitting at the table alone one night after dinner, James experienced a spiritual crisis of such proportions that he was reduced to an utter emotional wreck. Afterwards, his visits with local physicians were to no avail because there did not appear to be anything organically wrong; their only prescription for him was to frequent the baths, take the water cure, and hope that purgatives would cure his problem. While attending one of these local resorts, in absolute despair, he confided in a Mrs. Chichester the depths and blackness of his recent experience—his whole being now adrift in a dark sea—and his complete incomprehension as to what had happened. To his surprise, Mrs. Chichester gave the first sensible explanation he had heard, saying that what he had experienced was what Swedenborg called a "vastation," or complete emptying out of the contents of selfhood in preparation for receiving true spiritual sight. After her somewhat superficial sketch of Swedenborg's system, as he later recounted it, James, Sr., rushed out and purchased *Divine Love and Wisdom* and *True Christian Religion*. Devouring them immediately, he declared himself a convert.

Not long after this, probably through Carlyle, Henry James, Sr., met James John Garth Wilkinson. Wilkinson, in effect, became the equivalent of a pastoral psychiatrist, first to James the Elder and later to members of James's family. In appreciation for Wilkinson's aid at this crucial time, James named one of his sons Garth Wilkinson James

to honor his new friend. Wilkinson reciprocated by nam-
ing his own daughter Mary, after James's wife. Then, from
1846 to 1860, James financed Wilkinson's translations of
Swedenborg; he arranged for Wilkinson to become a foreign correspondent for the *New York Tribune* and a contributor to the Fourierist publication *The Harbinger.* James
also introduced Wilkinson to his American friends Henry
Wadsworth Longfellow, Charles Anderson Dana, and
Nathaniel Hawthorne; and he launched Wilkinson on the
public-lecture circuit by introducing Wilkinson's works to
the New Church in America. It was James who suggested
that Wilkinson turn to the practice of homeopathic medicine, and again it may have been James who helped
Wilkinson, already a member of the Royal College of Sur-
geons, to get a degree from the Philadelphia College of
Homeopathic Medicine. When Emerson went abroad in
1855, he met Wilkinson for the first time through James,
and the exchange that took place led to copies of Wilkinson's books in Emerson's personal library.[42]

The most notable influence of Henry James, Sr., and
James John Garth Wilkinson on Emerson in the late 1840s
can be found in the pages of Emerson's *Representative Men*
(1850).[43] In 1845, the year James returned from abroad,
Emerson began lecturing to public audiences on Swedenborg. It was the same lecture, polished over time with
each repetition, until 1850, when it appeared as chapter
3, "Swedenborg, the Mystic," in Emerson's collection of
distinguished portraits. Great men, Emerson said there,
are a window onto humanity. When they die, there is no
replacing them, for their class dies with them. Their
achievement, however, is in the awakening of humanity to
the possibilities they inspire; for, once seen, even the

meanest of us now know that the pinnacle can be reached. Swedenborg was our example of the genius who was inwardly oriented and who, in his writings, gave us a vision of our spiritual interiors.

While the members of the Swedenborgian church objected strenuously to Emerson's characterization of Swedenborg as a mystic, Emerson maintained that his use of the term meant Swedenborg stood for all those who look within because no other such personality type was represented in the remaining men of his book. Swedenborg's life, he said, was one worthy to be held up as a window into the world soul. Significantly, the details of Swedenborg's life Emerson culled exclusively from Wilkinson's then-recent biography of the Swedish seer, and much of the content of Swedenborg's books reported on by Emerson was taken from Wilkinson's translations of those works.

As for his assessment, while he exalted Swedenborg's life, Emerson was also equally critical of it. He was naturally attracted to the self-taught, intensely inward nature of Swedenborg's accomplishments. But, Emerson said, as he had elsewhere, that Swedenborg erred in assigning a fixed ecclesiastical meaning to each object. "The slippery," says Emerson, "is not so easily caught. In nature each individual symbol plays innumerable parts. . . , Nature is no literalist . . . , and she avenges herself on hard pedantry that would chain her waves." Swedenborg's "theological bias thus fatally narrowed his interpretation of nature, and the [great] dictionary of symbols is yet to be written. But the interpreter whom mankind still expects will find no precursor who has approached so near the true problem."

And finally, Emerson said:

> My concern is with the universal truth of Swedenborg's
> sentences, not at all with the circumstances or vocabu-
> lary. To seek too much of that were low and gossiping.
> He may and must speak to his circumstance and the
> way of events and belief around him, to Christendom
> or Islamism as his birth befell; he may speak of angels
> or Jews, or gods or Luthcrans or gypsies, or whatever
> figures come next to hand; I can readily enough trans-
> late his rhetoric into mine.[44]

Naturally, then, the diffusion of Swedenborgian ideas
throughout the transcendentalist community radiated
from the personality of Emerson himself. At Emerson's
behest, members of the loose-knit Transcendentalist Club
in Concord made a careful study of Swedenborg's major
theological works, including *True Christian Religion,
Heaven and Hell,* and *Conjugial Love.*[45] Thereafter, Swedenborg would occasionally come up, for instance, as a topic
in Bronson Alcott's famous conversations. Once, when Alcott contended that dark-skinned people were demonic
and blue-eyed blonds closest to God, someone in the audience reminded him that Swedenborg had said that Ne-
groes are the most beloved of all the races of heaven.[46]
Alcott, we also know, had read the works of Sampson
Reed and discussed Swedenborg with Emerson, after
which he attempted to apply Reed to the educational
classroom environment in his *Observations and Conversations with Children on the Gospels* (1836). Alcott's other
major work, *Orphic Sayings* (1841–42), borrowed in part

from Swedenborg's *True Christian Religion* and *Heaven and Hell.* His doctrine of the "Lapse from Grace" was also taken from Swedenborg.[47]

Thoreau and Theodore Parker read Swedenborg more lightly, if at all. Canby, in his biography of Thoreau, for instance, quotes a passage from Thoreau's journals, where Thoreau wished to record "the perfect correspondence of Nature to man, so that he is at home in her"; but Canby surmises that Thoreau was not adhering to a strict Swedenborgian meaning of correspondence.[48] Harding and Meyer state that Thoreau was probably most familiar with Swedenborg through conversations with Emerson, and they quote a letter that Thoreau wrote to B. B. Wiley, December 12, 1856, in which Thoreau states, "I cannot say that Swedenborg has been directly and practically valuable to me."[49]

James Freeman Clarke, who was also conversant in Swedenborg's works, went so far as to hire the Swedenborg Chapel in Boston, January 1841, in his attempt to form a new congregation of his own. Despite competing services held nearby by William Ellery Channing, Clarke spoke to a full house.[50] Another member of Emerson's circle, James Elliot Cabot, who, with Emerson and Parker, launched the *Massachusetts Quarterly Review* in 1847, in an opening statement boldly declared that one of the burning questions of the day was to settle Swedenborg's reputation. Frederick Henry Hedge, the German scholar of the group, had published an article on Swedenborg in the *Christian Examiner* as early as 1832, later claiming that it was one of the earliest published pieces to lean in the direction of transcendentalism.[51]

Julia Ward Howe, returning by ship from a holiday in Rome in 1851, on a month's voyage, occupied herself with, among other books, Swedenborg's *Divine Love and Wisdom* and later described the dawn of her new attitude toward Christianity as deriving from an understanding of Swedenborg's theory of the divine man, Parker's preaching, ideas discussed at the Boston Radical Club, and F. Ellingwood Abbott's comparison of Jesus with Socrates. These influences led her to conceive of Christ, she said, as "a Heavenly being whose presence was beneficence, whose word was judgement, whose brief career on earth through the body of Jesus ended in a sacrifice, whose purity and pathos have had much to do with the redemption of the human race from barbarism and the rule of the animal passions."[52] Lydia Maria Child, another relation of the Concord circle, was actually a member of the Boston Swedenborg Society beginning in 1821 but, by 1840, had become somewhat disappointed that the New Church did not take a more active part in social reform.[53]

In addition, Van Wyck Brooks recounts that William Dean Howells's father, of Welsh and Pennsylvania Dutch descent, was an ardent Swedenborgian, printer, and antislavery man who sympathized with Robert Dale Owen; was a friend of President Garfield; and often read aloud from Swedenborg's *Arcana*. Howells encouraged his son in a career of letters and had the kind of spiritual personality that understood well the daydreams of young William, toiling over a type case, spontaneously composing stories as he went along setting them up in print.[54]

The transcendentalists, in short, took up Swedenborg avidly and adapted him to their own individual purposes.

They saw him as comparable to other great mystical writers, such as Plotinus and Jakob Böhme, and believed him worthy of the same recognition as Immanuel Kant, Friedrich von Schelling, S. T. Coleridge, and W. E. Channing. They took him partly by way of protest against the prevailing secular materialism as well as the pretensions of ecclesiastical orthodoxy and partly as an affirmation of the divinity within each person. They saw in him a vast suggestiveness, and his ideas became part of the major reform movements of the times.

Nowhere is this spirit of reform more evident than in the Swedenborgian influence on Brook Farm, that idyllic experiment of a "perfected earth that shall at last bear on her bosom a race of men worthy of the name,"[55] whose great motto was "leisure to live in all faculties of the soul."[56] Brook Farm, of course, was the transcendentalist utopian experiment that lived and died on twenty-one acres of land in West Roxbury, Massachusetts, between 1841 and 1847. Born as the brainchild of George Ripley, a disaffected Unitarian minister and confidant of Emerson's inner circle, Brook Farm boasted such illustrious personalities in its heyday as Charles Anderson Dana, George William and James Burrill Curtis, John Sullivan Dwight, and Nathaniel Hawthorne (who shoveled manure in the mornings so he could "buy time to write" in the afternoons). Emerson, Fuller, Bronson Alcott, W. H. Channing, Orestes Brownson, Parker, and Christopher Cranch were among its distinguished visitors.[57]

As contemporary scholarship has it, the Brook Farm community began as a communal experiment to establish a heaven on earth of harmonious labor and intellect, the practical application of transcendentalist principles that sought to equalize the status of all tasks in society, while at the same time preserving the integrity of individual minds. It was later characterized as succeeding in spiritual vigor but failing because of economic ineptitude. While transcendentalist idealism sustained it in the beginning, some overall structure was eventually sought; and, in 1843, the community became an organized Fourierist phalanx. It was a remedy that one commentator has said eventually led to its ruin.

Two stages, then, can be identified with the formal period of Brook Farm's operation, but a look at the community's main publication, *The Harbinger*, during the full eight years of its operation, suggests a third phase, namely, Swedenborgian. While Swedenborgian ideas occasionally appeared in the literary output of *The Harbinger* during its first six years of operation, these ideas became more evident when, after the community closed in 1847 because of a major fire, *The Harbinger* moved to New York City and continued under the direction of Henry James, Sr., until 1849.[58]

A year later, in 1850, Emerson published his *Representative Men*, which brought to a close the forty-year era of his most extensive references to Swedenborg.[59] The saturation of transcendentalist thought with Swedenborgian ideas had by that time been accomplished, and its next phase would be a further diffusion throughout New England culture. One sure sign was the acquisition of Swedenborg's works by the Concord Public Library, all editions of which date from 1850 to 1900. Meanwhile, Swedenborgian churches flourished throughout the region and were supported by the wealth of famous New England families. When Harvard Divinity School declined funds to endow a chair in Swedenborgian studies, the Swedenborg School of Religion was founded in 1889 in Cambridge for the preparation of New Church ministers. The aging Thomas Worcester was its first president.

By that time, Swedenborgian interest in homeopathy was widespread in Massachusetts; and, in the 1890s, influential church members, such as Dr. Samuel Worcester, a Harvard Medical School graduate, prevailed upon the Massachusetts legislature to grant public tax money to open Westboro State Hospital, the first homeopathic insane asylum in the state.[60] By far, however, the greater diffusion of Swedenborgian ideas took place outside the institutional church, especially through the writings of the younger transcendentalists and in the practices of the American mental healers, who were the principal inheritors of an intuitive psychology of character formation that had been summarily abandoned by the scientific psychologists returning to America in droves from German universities in the closing decades of the nineteenth century.

Entwined as the Swedenborgian and transcendentalist impulses were, it is no wonder, with the passing of the Golden Age in Concord, that public interest in Swedenborg would also go into eclipse. Strange as it may seem, though the name of Swedenborg was so well known at the time, barely one hundred years later, in our own day, if any man or woman were asked, it is likely that fewer than one in a thousand would have ever even heard the name. Emerson, at least, fares a little better. Nevertheless, through a process that might be called the naturalization of ideas—in which specific intellectual influences have now become part of the flow of common culture, both

Swedenborgian and transcendentalist thought survive as integral, albeit hidden, strands of the fabric that defines present-day folk consciousness in America.

## Notes

1. The biographical material here and following has been adapted from Oliver Wendell Holmes, *Ralph Waldo Emerson: A Memoir* (Boston: Houghton Mifflin, 1884); James Elliot Cabot, *A Memoir of Ralph Waldo Emerson*, 2 vols. (Boston: Houghton Mifflin, 1888); and Gay Wilson Allen, *Waldo Emerson: A Biography* (New York: Viking Press, 1981).

2. Sampson Reed, *A Biological Sketch of Thomas Worcester, D.D.* (Boston: Massachusetts New Church Union, 1880).

3. Reed quotes Worcester on the title, probably *Arcana Coelestia*.

4. Ralph Waldo Emerson, *Letters*, ed. Ralph Rusk, 6 vols. (New York: Columbia University Press, 1939), vol. 3, p. 74.

5. Ibid., vol. 1, p. 306.

6. Perry Miller, *The Transcendentalists: An Anthology* (Cambridge: Harvard University Press, 1950), p. 50.

7. Sampson Reed, "Oration on Genius," in Elizabeth Palmer Peabody, ed., *Aesthetic Papers* (New York: G. P. Putnam, 1849), pp. 58–63.

8. Ralph Waldo Emerson, *Journals*, ed. E. W. Emerson and W. E. Forbes, 10 vols. (Boston: Houghton Mifflin, 1909), vol. 2, p. 25.

9. Holmes, *Emerson*, p. 41.

10. Sampson Reed, *Observations on the Growth of the Mind*, with a biographical preface by James Reed (Boston: Houghton Mifflin, 1886; first published, 1826).

11. Emerson, *Journals*, vol. 2, pp. 116–117.

12. Emerson, *Letters*, vol 1, p. 173.

13. Ibid., p. 176.

14. Emerson, *Journals*, vol. 2, p. 124.

15. Emerson, *Letters*, vol. 1, p. 273, n. 21.

16. Emerson, *Journals*, vol. 2, p. 164.

17. Ibid., pp. 455–456, for instance.

18. Ibid., pp. 500–501.

19. Ibid., p. 266.

20. Ralph Waldo Emerson to Thomas Carlyle, 14 May 1834, in *The Correspondence of Thomas Carlyle and Ralph Waldo Emerson, 1834–1372*, 2 vols. (Boston: Houghton Mifflin, 1883), pp. 16–17.

21. Carlyle to Emerson, 12 August 1834, ibid., vol. 1, p. 19.

22. Emerson to Carlyle, 20 November 1834, ibid., p. 32.

23. Ibid.

24. Reed, *Growth of the Mind* (1886), p. ix.

25. Emerson, *Journals*, vol. 3, p. 432.

26. Cabot, *A Memoir*, vol. 1, p. 259.

27. Holmes, *Emerson*, vol. 1, p. 93.

28. Ibid., pp. 79–81. See also the introduction to Emerson's *Nature, Addresses, Lectures*, ed. R. E. Spiller and A. R. Ferguson (Cambridge: Harvard University Press, 1979), pp. ix–6; and M. R. Konvitz, ed. *The Recognition of Ralph Waldo Emerson: Selected Criticism since 1837* (Ann Arbor: University of Michigan Press, 1972), pp. ix–xiii.

29. Culled at random from Emerson, *Nature*.

30. See, for instance, Paul F. Boller, Jr., *American Transcendentalism, 1830–1860: An Intellectual Inquiry* (New York: G. P. Putnam, 1974), which has a discussion on Emerson's use of the term *correspondence*.

31. Emerson, *Journals*, vol. 4, pp. 36–38; 131–132.

32. Emerson, *Letters*, vol. 1, p. 173, ed. n. 21.

33. Henry James, Sr., "Emerson," *The Atlantic Monthly* 96 (1904): 741.

34. Quoted in Ralph Barton Perry, *The Thought and Character of William James* (Boston: Little, Brown, 1931), vol. 1, pp. 39–41.

35. Austin Warren, *Henry James the Elder* (New York: Macmillan, 1934), p. 43.

36. Ibid.

37. Ibid, pp. 44–45.

38. Ibid, p. 47.

39. Ibid, p. 48.

40. Allen, *Waldo Emerson*, p. 401.

41. Warren, *Henry James*, p. 46.

42. See, for instance, only a partial listing in Walter Harding, *Emerson's Library* (Charlottesville, VA: University of Virginia Press, 1967), p. 301; and a more complete list of references in R. K. Silver, "The Spiritual Kingdom in America: The Influence of Emanuel Swedenborg on American Society and Culture, 1816–1860," Ph.D. diss. (Stanford, 1983; Ann Arbor, MI: University Microfilms).

43. Ralph Waldo Emerson, *Representative Men: Seven Lectures* (Boston: Houghton Mifflin, 1887; originally published, 1850).

44. Quoted in Clarence Paul Hotson, "Sampson Reed, a Teacher of Emerson," *New England Quarterly* 2, no. 2 (April 1929): 272.

45. Silver, "Spiritual Kingdom," p. 88.

46. Martha Saxton, *Louisa May: A Modern Biography of Louisa May Alcott* (Boston: Houghton Mifflin, 1977), p. 122.

47. Silver, "Spiritual Kingdom," p. 101. Silver also says that Margaret Fuller reported a number of conversations with Emerson and Alcott on the subject of Swedenborg. Fuller was familiar with some of

Swedenborg's books as well as articles about him, and many of her critical pieces in *The Dial* borrowed from Swedenborg's ideas of correspondences and universal order. The Concord poet Christopher Cranch also borrowed his ideas of analogy and correspondences from Swedenborg. Cranch had read parts of the *Arcana* and used the correspondence theory to write poetry for *The Dial.* Silver, "Spiritual Kingdom," p. 99.

48. Henry S. Canby, *Thoreau* (Boston: Houghton Mifflin, 1939), p. 421.

49. W. Harding and M. Meyer, *The New Thoreau Handbook* (New York: New York University Press, 1980), p. 98.

50. E. E. Hale, ed., *James Freeman Clarke: Autobiography, Diary, and Correspondence* (Boston: Houghton Mifflin, 1891), pp. 156–157.

51. G. W. Cooke, *An Historical and Biographical Introduction to Accompany "The Dial,"* 2 vols. (New York: Russell & Russell, 1961), vol. 1, p. 191; vol. 2, p. 73.

52. Julia Ward Howe, *Reminiscences, 1819–1899* (Boston: Houghton Mifflin, 1899), pp. 204, 208.

53. Cooke, *Historical and Biographical Introduction*, pp. 166–167. Cooke also reports that William Henry Channing, in his publication *The Present,* wrote several articles on Swedenborg.

54. Van Wyck Brooks, *New England Indian Summer, 1865–1915* (New York: Dutton, 1940), pp. 40–41.

55. Lindsay Swift, *Brook Farm: Its Members, Scholars, and Visitors* (Secaucus, NJ: Citadel Press, 1973; first published in 1900).

56. Ibid.

57. Ibid.

58. The most notable convert who actually took part in the utopian experiment was Warren Burton, a Harvard classmate of Emerson's and Unitarian minister in East Cambridge, who joined Brook Farm in 1841 and, as a result of interest among its members in Swedenborg's writings, switched denominations and joined the New Church. Swift, *Brook Farm*, pp. 194–198.

59. Scattered references to Swedenborg do occur in Emerson's journals after 1850, mainly comparing him to other writers on the nature of inner experience.

60. For more on the diffusion of the Swedenborgian influence in the late nineteenth century, but with an emphasis on the growth of the Swedenborgian church, see Marguerite Block, *New Church in the New World* (New York: Swedenborg Foundation, 1978).

D. T. SUZUKI

# *Suzuki*
# *on Swedenborg*

## BY D. T. SUZUKI

Translation and Introduction by Kei Torita

## *Introduction*

Daisetz T. Suzuki (1870–1966), internationally known as a Buddhist scholar and the man who introduced Zen Buddhism to the West, is also known among Swedenborgians as the philosopher who introduced Swedenborg to the East.

After receiving a degree in philosophy from Tokyo University, Suzuki lived in the United States for many years. From 1897 to 1907, he lived in LaSalle, Illinois, where he worked as the editor of Oriental Studies for the Open Court Publishing Company and where he first began reading Swedenborg. In 1911, now back in Japan, he married an American woman, Beatrice Elizabeth Lane, a graduate of Radcliffe College and Columbia University.

In 1908, the London-based Swedenborg Society asked Suzuki to translate Swedenborg's *Heaven and Hell* into Japanese, which was published in 1910. Subsequently, Suzuki also translated *The New Jerusalem and Its Heavenly*

*Doctrine* (1914), *Divine Love and Wisdom* (1914), and *Divine Providence* (1915). Suzuki, incidentally, translated Swedenborg's text from English translations, not from the original Latin.

So, it was during an intensive-five year period that Suzuki actively studied and translated Swedenborg. During this time, in 1914, he also wrote and published a book titled *Suedenborugu*. *Suedenborugu* is primarily a biography, but it contains other elements as well, as if Suzuki wanted to include as much information as possible in a single volume to impress Swedenborg and his theological ideas on a wide Japanese audience. While presenting Swedenborg's life, Suzuki also includes long explanations of Swedenborg's doctrines, excerpts from his writings, whole outlines or tables of contents of works, and letters and published materials from Swedenborg's contemporaries.

In *Suedenborugu*, we also find most of Suzuki's personal response to Swedenborg. A devout Buddhist all of his life, Suzuki, nevertheless, seems to have found in Swedenborg a connection between the Swede's eighteenth-century Christian approach to life and to God and his own. We find Suzuki praising not only Swedenborg's scientific genius and spiritual vision but also his work ethic, his style of living, his love of country, his gentleness toward others, even his abstinence from eating meat. Indeed, in chapter 6, Suzuki devotes a long passage to Swedenborg's breathing techniques, a matter of serious concern for this dedicated Buddhist. Suzuki even seems to understand and to feel the anxiety Swedenborg must have felt in accepting his spiritual calling. In some places, Suzuki seems to think of Swedenborg as a Buddhist scholar or a perfect Japanese gentleman.

I have translated those sections that capture Swedenborg the person. I have included most of *Suedenborugu*'s
long first chapter, which explains Suzuki's reasons for this
undertaking; much of the second chapter, which contains
Swedenborg's spiritual awakening; and those parts of the
succeeding chapters that capture Suzuki's personal assessment of the man and the theologian. I have made no attempt to present this picture in full, but offer it as
snapshots of a brief but intense (and highly personal) relationship.

Suzuki's professional preoccupation with Swedenborg
was brief, ending in 1915; after that time, Suzuki barely
mentioned the Swedish mystic's name in his writings.
However, there is evidence that Swedenborg remained in
Suzuki's thoughts, as this note that Suzuki wrote to a
friend in 1953 (when Suzuki was 83 years old) suggests:

> Professor Benz [of Marburg University] talked about
> interesting material on [Meister] Echart today. The
> professor wrote a book on Swedenborg recently
> [1948]. Since I am still interested in Swedenborg, we
> enjoyed our conversation.

In translating this work, I used *Suzuki Daisetz Zenshu*
(Collected Works of Daisetz Suzuki), ed. Shokin Furuta,
vol. 24 (Tokyo: Iwanami Publishing Company, 1982). It is
written in old Japanese, which is difficult for a Japanese
reader of the late twentieth century to use. I have, however, remained faithful to Suzuki's content and style,
using freer translations only when dictionaries did not
help.

KEI TORITA
Tokyo, Japan

# *From* Suedenborugu *by D.T. Suzuki*

### *Preface*

Theological revolutionary, traveler of heaven and hell, expert on the spiritual world, great king of the mystical realm, seer unique throughout history, scholar of incomparable energy, clear-minded scientist, gentleman free from worldly desires—all of these make Swedenborg. In our nation today [Japan in 1913], the religious and ideological field is finally opened to new influences. Those who are concerned about society today should know this man.

This is why this book is written.

### *Chapter 1*

Swedenborg's name is hardly known in [Japan]. . . . And among those who have heard of him, there would be only a few who believe that this man has much relevance to current culture and thought. They might simply regard him as an example of an unusual psychology and, therefore, reduce him to a case study in that field. But anyone who studies Swedenborg seriously would find that he is an interesting subject for study in many ways.

First of all, Swedenborg says that he traveled in heaven and hell and actually saw the state of human beings after death. His statements are sincere and not exaggerated. If we consider them in light of common sense, we find they ring true. This is the first reason that I consider Swedenborg interesting.

It seems that there is a spiritual world aside from the world of our five senses. When we enter into a certain kind of psychological state, we are able to get in touch with this spiritual realm. Even if we did not see any moral connections between such other-worldly circumstances and those of this world, these revelations would still be of interest from scientific and philosophical viewpoints. This is the second reason for studying Swedenborg.

Swedenborg's theological doctrine is very similar to that of Buddhism: that we must leave *proprium* [illusion of self-guidance]; that salvation is based on the harmony between faith and practice; that the Divine is wisdom and love itself, yet love is higher and deeper than wisdom; that divine providence prevails over everything, great and small; that nothing in the world is accidental [because] divine providence is contained in every iota, in which the actualization of love and wisdom is recognizable. Any of these points would intrigue scholars of religion, especially Buddhists. This is the third reason that Swedenborg should be studied.

In addition to these three points, . . . the unique quality of Swedenborg's personality makes me feel that he should not be neglected. A wonderful combination of scientific and religious talents constituted his personality. Such a remarkable person is good material for psychological study, but he also provides a good example: his energetic yet unworldly life provides us with lessons in how to live.

Reading his writings, considering his life, and examining his thoughts, we feel as if Swedenborg himself emerges before our eyes. Here we see an elderly, dignified gentleman. Even though his body is physically in this world, his "inner" eyes are always filled with heavenly mysteries. He appears to walk in the clouds and to hear heavenly music. If anyone asks this gentleman about the path to heaven, he answers him without interruption, as an inexhaustible stream; and yet expresses nothing strange or disturbing. He speaks as plainly as if he were speaking about the things in the world of the five senses. Some things leave his listeners amazed or bewildered. Yet the elderly man regards all he says with the same calmness as [if he were speaking of] everyday affairs. This is why he is difficult to understand.

If such is Swedenborg and such his doctrine, he ought to be known to the world. He ought to be taught to us like Kant and Wesley, his contemporaries. Why, then, is his doctrine known only to a few people? There are two main reasons.

First, his writing style is too repetitious—as if an old man were teaching children. In general, however, whether or not someone's name is known to later generations is not always based on whether or not his thoughts are lofty [but on whether his style is pleasing]. . . .

The second reason is that what he describes belongs to other worlds, apart from our world of five senses, and ordinary people find many of his statements unbelievable. Moreover, he speaks about such things in such a matter-of-fact tone, without any exaggeration, that it may cast doubt [on his experiences]. . . .

If we add a third reason, it is that his description seems much too detailed. When Swedenborg is dealing with matters that transcend common sense, too much detail in description may, contrary to his intention, provoke disbelief. . . .

These are, however, trivial points after all is said and done. We should not doubt his overall credibility and rationality because of these points. What he says is coherent and sincere. He doesn't lie; he merely describes what he has seen and heard without any affectation. Whether or not we believe what he says, there must be a reason for such straightforwardness. That reason itself is worth thorough study. Since this fact concerns our moral and religious life, we must not neglect it. . . .

## *Chapter 2*

[After recounting Swedenborg's childhood, university experience, scientific studies and travels abroad, work as a Swedish mining official, and early scientific publications, Suzuki arrives at Swedenborg's life in the year 1744, when he first began his mystical encounters.]

The thirteen-year period between the publication of *Principia* and that of *The Animal Kingdom* allowed Swedenborg to study the structure of the human body and step at last into the spiritual world.

*Economy of the Animal Kingdom* and *The Animal Kingdom* were the last publications of his secular life. Although he still had some unpublished manuscripts, he did not wish to publish anything except for these two works because, soon after that, he had a unique spiritual experience, from which time his life totally changed. He regarded his former studies in philosophy and science as something apart from God's will, not his true calling. He assumed an entirely new attitude. Still, in my opinion, there is no unbridgeable gap between his so-called secular life and his later spiritual life. It would appear that the thoughts and feelings of his former intellectual concerns were always recognizable. . . .

[Here Suzuki presents the prologue to *The Animal Kingdom*, which sets down Swedenborg's design to examine human anatomy in order to "open all the doors that lead to . . . the soul herself . . ."]

We can see that the spiritual experiences of the latter half of Swedenborg's life cannot be basically separated from the intellectual study of his earlier life. It is often said that, in 1744, when he was 56 years old, he had a spiritual experience and he entered a new life. Yet, this life is not totally unrelated [to his past]; and I cannot help but regard this new life as, in a way, only a continuation and development of the first half. It may be, however, that his so-called "soul's own contemplation" was not necessarily what he expected; but this does not matter from the standpoint of the development of his entire life.

Trying to study the life of the soul itself from an intellectual and analytical approach, Swedenborg first made attempts through chemistry, physiology, and human anatomy, to which he devoted all his extraordinary genius so that he might somehow unravel the mystery of the soul. In his heart, however, he was still not satisfied. As a result of this concentrated study, his inner sight gradually opened, and he was equipped with a mysterious power to enter the spiritual world on his own. Swedenborg himself regards this power as God's special will. His followers also regard this experience as Swedenborg's receiving unusual divine grace and believe that no technique or study can produce such a result again. I, however, secretly feel that this is not necessarily true.

Swedenborg wrote one work during the transitional

period between his intellectual life and his spiritual life. *The Worship and Love of God* was published in London in 1745. In this book, Swedenborg no longer uses a mathematical style, as in *The Principia*, but rather describes the creation of the universe from both an artistic and philosophical viewpoint. He regards God as the source of all sciences and believes that the traces of wisdom in the universe depend upon divine providence and an "original vow of salvation" [Suzuki here uses the Buddhist term *hongan*]. Swedenborg's thoughts and feelings are more and more clearly religious, so that they are expressed almost in the manner of a religious scholar. The spirituality of his later life did not come accidentally; it came gradually, step by step, as if a tree sprouted, put forth leaves, blossomed, and produced fruit. Indeed, his spirituality seems to have come naturally. Of course, the result might have looked quite different from what had been expected, but that does not negate its natural maturation.

[In 1744], Swedenborg was an extraordinary scientific genius. He not only set forth unprecedented theories in mining, mathematics, engineering, crystallography, astronomy, etc., but he also had far-sighted views on anatomy, psychology, and philosophy, many of which were precursors of those held today. This is all known to current experts in these areas, and I need not elaborate on this subject. But more than this, it is the second half of his life that made Swedenborg what he was, in which he realized his true calling, that has granted him a special position in the religious world and has provided hitherto unknown subjects of psychological study. Once he began a new life, he abandoned all his desire for scientific knowledge, all his former intellectual pursuits, and devoted his talents and spirit to his spiritual life. In this new life is found the main purpose of my writing this book. Without the latter half of his life, Swedenborg would have been admired by later generations only as an outstanding scientist. Divine providence always surprises us humans. No matter is settled until the coffin is closed.

## Chapter 3

Swedenborg's spiritual experience did not begin suddenly but rather came gradually. Therefore, there was no particular day that he entered his new life. Having experience after experience, he finally made up his mind to give up his former intellectual life. Of course, he had much pain and struggle until then. . . . While it does not appear that he experienced indecision in giving up his former scholarly life, other accounts tell that he could not help but agonizing day and night for a while after a spiritual encounter.

Because of his scientific genius and scholarship and his renown in these areas, others placed much hope in him for the future. We can imagine how deep was Swedenborg's inner pain and struggle, to renounce all fame in these areas overnight and to become a kind of instrument to deliver God's revelations as they came, without depending on his own efforts and intelligence. It would be like a Buddhist who believes in salvation by his own efforts converting to one who believes in salvation by another. Believing in salvation by another sounds easy, but its penance is just as hard as self-reliance. This is well known to those who live the religious life.

[Suzuki discusses *Arcana Coelestia*, Swedenborg's first

work after his spiritual awakening and then remarks on Swedenborg's continued diligence in public affairs, a trait Suzuki admired greatly in the Swedish seer.]

What is noteworthy . . . is that, in spite of the fact that Swedenborg was involved in such voluminous writing, he fulfilled his responsibility as a member of the Swedish House of Nobles by presenting his considered opinions, without hesitation, on Sweden's financial affairs. Moreover, these opinions were not vague, fanciful, abstract theories so often made by scholars or religious thinkers, but each was a concrete policy appropriate to the time. . . .

[Here follows a long discussion of Swedenborg's important spiritual works, including *Heaven and Hell, The Last Judgment, Divine Love and Wisdom,* and *Divine Providence,* when Suzuki again takes up the subject of Swedenborg's diligence.]

His manuscripts are in folio, written in very small and neat letters; and his penmanship is extremely beautiful. Imagine an elderly man in his seventies, even in his eighties, industriously engaged in such writing every day. To publish them, he left his homeland to go to Holland and to England without a day to rest. His example would shame today's lazy scholars into hiding from him.

## Chapter 4

. . . If Swedenborg had wished to get wealth and fame by his mystical powers, it could have been possible because it is an undeniable fact that he actually had such mysterious interactions. However, in pursuing his lofty mission, he did not demonstrate such power in an unworthy manner. . . . He stated, "The reason that I am permitted to communicate with the spiritual world is that God has something particular to command me [to accomplish]. There is no doubt about this. To please the minds of worldly people in vain is to forget the great purpose of my mission. That is not the will of Heaven." [Suzuki then quotes a long section of Immanuel Kant's letter to Charlotte von Knoblock, written in 1763, concerning a story about Swedenborg and a fire in Stockholm, in which Kant concludes:]

> There are some more episodes to prove that Swedenborg had spiritual sight. But since what he really is does not depend on such things, I will not go into details. Suffice it to say that he had this ability.

## Chapter 5

[Suzuki opens this chapter with remarks on Swedenborg's physical appearance and then goes on to remark on his personality and other aspects of his life.]

It would have been easy for a person who had traveled around heaven and hell and had received a mission directly from God to be arrogant, narrow-minded, and rude, unsociable toward others. But, to the contrary, Swedenborg was innocent, even childlike or like a mystic who is unsoiled by the world. . . .

Although not exactly a vegetarian, he was not much fond of meat; he seems to have regarded eating meat as incompatible with heavenly doctrine. . . . It appears that meat-eating and noble thoughts do not go together. . . .

It was a remarkable fact that Swedenborg was not attached to money. . . . He was very independent on this matter. . . . Nor did he like lending money or giving alms.

. . . It seems that he thought lending money meant losing money. Also, because he needed to use all his income for his travels and publications, he never lent nor borrowed money. So, then, was he strict in money matters? Not at all. For instance, when his landlord asked for the rent, Swedenborg sent the man to his cashbox, telling him to take the money out of it. Whoever had money exchanges with him said that he was generous.

The amount of Swedenborg's writing over 63 years is amazingly enormous. . . . And each of these works is profound in thought, not something produced overnight. . . . In addition, it is marvelous that all his works were done by himself, without a secretary or scribe and that each book is arranged in an orderly fashion, without any confusion. Because he had made a kind of index from the outset, as he wrote one volume after another, he did not make mistakes in referring to works previously published but was able to preserve his system. . . .

## Chapter 6

I will not discuss whether Swedenborg's experiences of traveling through heaven and hell were accomplished by God's secret will since it is not the purpose of this book. However, this kind of experience seems to have a lot to do with breathing. Swedenborg himself made an in-depth study of breathing techniques. According to his doctrine of correspondence, the lungs in the human body correspond to intellect, while the heart corresponds to love; and the spiritual relationship between wisdom and love are similar to the physical relationship between the lungs and the heart. If we know the one, we can understand the other. Therefore, to control our breathing means to improve our intelligence. There are internal and external kinds of breathing: the latter comes from our earthly world; the former, from the spiritual world. When a person dies, his external breathing stops, but his silent, internal breathing never ceases. While we have our physical existence, our internal breathing is too quiet to hear. This breathing is the spiritual life coming forth from the true inside in one's spirit. It is this internal breathing that enables one to communicate with the spiritual. . . .

Swedenborg could differentiate between internal and external breathing, but not all of us can perceive the difference. It seems unquestionable, however, that controlling our breathing has much to do with the discipline of mind and body. Swedenborg's ability [to control his breathing], almost from birth, may have had some significance in his later mission. . . .

As we can see from even these brief extracts of *Suedenborugu*, Suzuki's fascination with Swedenborg went far beyond a mere translation of a Western theologian's writings into Japanese. The Buddhist master seems to have felt a kinship with the Swedish seer. As Shokin Furuta, the editor of Suzuki's collected works and his disciple, has commented in his radio lectures on Suzuki:

> Dr. Suzuki's conclusion of Buddhist scholarship seems to be that the fundamentals of Buddhism can be summarized as "Great Wisdom" and "Great Mercy." I suppose this was somehow suggested from Swedenborg's concept of Divinity, that is, Divine Love and Divine Wisdom.

# About
# the Contributors

**Jorge Luis Borges** was a perennial candidate for the Nobel Prize in literature and received numerous literary honors during his lifetime, among them the *Gran Premio Nacional de la Literatura* (Argentina, 1957); the *Prix Formentor* of the International Congress of Publishers (1961); and the prestigious Cervantes Prize (Spain, 1980). At first primarily a poet, he later became best known for his short stories. His first short story, one of his greatest works, was "Pierre Menard, Author of Don Quijote." His metaphysical themes and stylistic innovations have inspired younger generations to explore the realities of their rapidly evolving societies with far greater concern for universal and aesthetic values than did their predecessors. By introducing imagination as the chief fictional ingredient, thereby rescuing Latin and South American literature from dry, documentary realism, Borges gave birth to a new genre of literature: Magical Realism. Borges died in 1986.

**Czeslaw Milosz** has emerged as a preeminent voice of conscience for the twentieth century. A Lithuanian-born poet, novelist, essayist, translator, critic, and literary scholar who writes in Polish, Milosz received the Nobel Prize for literature in 1980 and the Neustadt International Prize for literature in 1978. Milosz is considered as a founder of the catastrophist school of Polish poetry. Yet, his work shows a strong propensity for spiritual themes as well as a deep admiration for those visionaries who lift the level of perception to salvatory realms of sanity. He claims his most important sources of inspiration are Swedenborg; Simone Weil; Dostoevsky; Blake; and his own distant cousin, Oscar V. de L. Milosz. Among his works available in English are *Emperor of the Earth: Modes of Eccentric Vision*; *The Rising of the Sun*; and *Unattainable Earth*.

**Kathleen Raine** is a poet, critic, translator, and editor who was educated at Girton College, Cambridge, England. Among her many publications are the two-volume *Blake and Tradition* (also published in a shorter version as *Blake and Antiquity*); *Defending Ancient Springs*; *William Blake*; and *Yeats the Initiate: Essays on Certain Themes in the Work of W. B. Yeats*. Her books of poetry include *Stone and Flower: Poems, 1935–43*; *The Lost Country*; *The Oval Portrait and Other Poems*; and *The Presence: Poems 1984–1989*.

**Colin Wilson** is regarded as a preeminent British writer on the subject of spirituality and the esoteric. His work includes nonfiction, novels, biographies, plays, and encyclopedic investigations of crimes and the occult. His seminal first work, *The Outsider*, written when he was just 24 years old, is considered a classic in the field. Among his other works are *Religion and the Rebel; Bernard Shaw: A Reassessment; Lord of the Underworld: Jung and the Twentieth Century;* and *The Misfits: A Study of Sexual Outsiders.*

**Wilson Van Dusen** is a natural scholar whose interests lie between religion and psychology. With a Ph.D. in clinical psychology, he worked for many years with the mentally ill, including as the chief psychologist at the Mendocino State Mental Hospital in California. Now retired from his professional practice, he has recently written a work that presents a unified view of the world's mystics. Van Dusen's most popular books are *The Natural Depth in Man* and *The Presence of Other Worlds,* a work devoted to Swedenborg, whom Van Dusen regards as a "colleague and companion."

**Eugene Taylor** received his A.B. and M.A. from Southern Methodist University and his Ph.D. from Boston University. From 1977–1979, he held Ralph Waldo Emerson's old position of Resident Graduate at the Harvard Divinity School. He is currently historian in Psychiatry at the Massachusetts General Hospital, a lecturer on Psychiatry at the Harvard Medical School, and director of the Cambridge Institute of Psychology and Religion. He has published numerous works, including *William James on Exceptional Mental States: Reconstruction of the Unpublished 1896 Lowell Lectures* and *Life of the Spirit: Talks on Psychology and Religion from the Swedenborg Chapel.*

**Daisetsu Teitaro Suzuki** is credited with introducing the West to Zen Buddhism. Born in 1870 in Toyko and brought up in a devotely Buddhist family, Suzuki pursued his religious and philosophical studies at Toyko University. After a ten-year sojourn in the United States, where he worked as an editor of Oriental Studies for Open Court Press, Suzuki returned to his native Japan where he undertook the translation of Swedenborg's works into Japanese. Throughout his long life (Suzuki died in 1966, at the age of 96), this Buddhist scholar taught at colleges in Japan, the United States, and Europe, including Cornell, Yale, Harvard, Cambridge, and Oxford. His works are collected in the 32-volume *Suzuki Daisetz Zenshu* (Tokyo: 1982). Among his works available in English are *Living by Zen* and *Mysticism: Christian and Buddhist, the Eastern and Western Way.*